SEC

SU

THE FASCINATING TALE OF AN AMAZING FEAT OF ENGINEERING

NATIONAL
GEOGRAPHIC
WASHINGTON, D.C.

CRET
BWAY

WITHDRAWN

BY MARTIN W. SANDLER

Fitchburg Public Library
5530 Lacy Road
Fitchburg, WI 53711

For Carol

I am deeply indebted to Virginia "Ginny" Koeth for invaluable aid in shaping this book and for the guidance she gave me. I am also most grateful for the vital contributions Amy Shields made to this volume and for the guidance she also gave me. And I am most appreciative of the marvelous job of picture research that Annette Keisow accomplished and the beautiful design that David Seager brought to the book. Many thanks are also due to my Jill-of-All-Trades Katherine Worten, and my agent John Thornton. And, as always, Carol Sandler has contributed more than words can express.

Text copyright © 2009 Martin W. Sandler
Published by the National Geographic Society
All rights reserved. Reproduction of the whole or any part of the contents
without written permission from the National Geographic Society is prohibited.

Book design by David M. Seager

Library of Congress Cataloging-in-Publication Data

Sandler, Martin W.
Secret subway / By Martin W. Sandler.
p. cm.
Includes bibliographical references and index.
ISBN 978-1-4263-0462-0 (hardcover : alk. paper) -- ISBN 978-1-4263-0463-7 (library binding : alk. paper)
1. Subways--New York (State)--New York. 2. New York (N.Y.)--History. I. Title.
TF847.N5S25 2009
388.4'28097471--dc22
2008039831

Founded in 1888, the National Geographic Society is one of the largest nonprofit scientific and educational organizations in the world.
It reaches more than 285 million people worldwide each month through its official journal, NATIONAL GEOGRAPHIC, and its four other magazines; the National
Geographic Channel; television documentaries; radio programs; films; books; videos and DVDs; maps; and interactive media. National Geographic has funded more than
8,000 scientific research projects and supports an education program combating geographic illiteracy.

For more information, please call 1-800-NGS LINE (647-5463) or write to the following address:

NATIONAL GEOGRAPHIC SOCIETY
1145 17th Street N.W.
Washington, D.C. 20036-4688 U.S.A.
Visit us online at www.nationalgeographic.com/books

For librarians and teachers: www.ngchildrensbooks.org
More for kids from National Geographic: kids.nationalgeographic.com
For information about special discounts for bulk purchases, please contact
National Geographic Books Special Sales: ngspecsales@ngs.org
For rights or permissions inquiries, please contact National Geographic Books Subsidiary Rights: ngbookrights@ngs.org

Printed in U.S.A.

CONTENTS

1 BIG CITY, BIG PROBLEM 7

2 ENTER ALFRED BEACH 19

3 "LIKE A SAIL-BOAT BEFORE THE WIND" 29

4 OVERCOMING BOSS TWEED 41

5 BUILDING THE SUBWAY 51

6 THE SUBWAY REVEALED 61

7 THE END OF TWEED 71

8 NEW YORK GETS ITS SUBWAY 79

Further Reading 92
Sources 92
Illustration Credits 94
Index 95

BIG CITY, BIG PROBLEM

As this photograph from the 1860s shows, New York City had become a world center for industry, commerce, and communication. "For better or for worse," one visitor wrote, "New York is fast becoming . . . America."

"THE STREETS ARE ALIVE WITH BUSINESS, RETAIL AND WHOLESALE, AND present an aspect of universal bustle. Flags are to be seen in every direction, the tall masts in the harbor appear above the houses . . . There are stores of the magnitude of bazaars . . . huge hotels, coffee houses, and places of amusement. [There] are palatial residences...railway whistles and steamboat bells [and] telegraph wires, eight to ten to a post . . ." That is how an English visitor to New York City in the 1850s described what she encountered there. A few years later a newspaper would exclaim, "It is the desire of every American to see New York, the largest and most wonderful city in the nation."

They were not exaggerations. By the 1860s, New York City had become one of the most exciting places in the world. More than 700,000 people lived there, and thousands of others were taking up residence every month. Tens of thousands of visitors poured into the city every year—and with good reason. Nowhere else were there so many elegant shops and department stores. Many of New York's restaurants rivaled the best that the proudest cities of Europe had to offer. Museums, libraries, and other cultural institutions abounded. And for fun seekers, New York, with its music halls, night-clubs, and theaters, was an entertainment paradise.

Among New York's greatest marvels was the first department store built in America. Created by merchant Alexander Stewart, the Marble Palace, as it came to be called, was five stories high, was constructed of dazzling white marble, had 5,000 feet of counter space on the first floor alone, and could accommodate 50,000 customers a day. Visitors, used to shopping in specialty shops where only one kind of merchandise was sold, were amazed at the overwhelming variety and abundance of goods that could be purchased under this one great roof. "It is spacious and magnificent," stated one New York politician, "beyond anything of the kind in the New World or the old . . ." Within a decade, New York's main thoroughfares would be lined with other department stores, each trying to outdo the others.

Increasingly, these same thoroughfares had become filled with hotels, many of them built on a grand scale to accommodate the hordes of visitors and businesspeople who poured into the city from around the world. "The entrances to these hotels invariably attract the eye . . ." one observer would write. "Groups are always lounging on the door-steps . . . There are southerners . . . smoking Havana cigars . . . Englishmen, shrouded in exclusiveness, who look on all their neighbors as so many barbarian intruders on their privacy; and people of all nations whom business had drawn to the American metropolis."

Many of the visitors had indeed been drawn to New York for business reasons, but tens of thousands of others came to be entertained. The city's theaters contained something for everyone. For the more affluent and serious-minded there were elegant opera houses and concert halls that featured performances by the world's greatest musical artists. For the common folk there were scores of popular theaters offering melodramas, variety shows, comedy, and burlesque. And there were certain attractions that could be found only in New York.

Chief among them was Barnum's American Museum, run by one of the greatest showmen and promoters of all time. Explaining his reason for creating his establishment, P. T. Barnum stated, "I meant to make people talk about

New York's streets were crowded almost beyond description. This is an artist's depiction of the scene outside Barnum's Museum.

my Museum, to exclaim over its wonders, to have men and women all over the country say: 'There is not another place in the United States where so much can be seen for twenty-five cents as in Barnum's American Museum.'"

Barnum accomplished all that—and more. His museum was unlike anything anyone had ever witnessed. Inside the vast building visitors encountered more than 500,000 natural and artificial curiosities from around the globe. Included were such diverse amazements as educated performing fleas, a dog who operated a knitting machine, a bearded woman, giants, dwarfs, jugglers, ventriloquists, and rope dancers. On the more serious side, there were fine paintings, rare stuffed animals from even the most remote countries, and dioramas and panoramas of famous historical events.

Among Barnum's main attractions were what he called "the Fiji mermaid" (it was a fake), a pair of Siamese twins (they were real), and a 25-inch midget named Tom Thumb who became a national celebrity. All combined to make the American Museum an enormous success. By the time Barnum's first museum burned down in 1865 and its successor, which was quickly built, was also destroyed by fire three years later, Barnum had sold some 42 million tickets. That was 7 million more than the entire population of the United States.

Department stores, restaurants, theaters, hotels, one-of-a-kind museums—New York had it all. But it was not only these attractions that made the city such a unique and vital place. By the mid-1860s it had also become the nation's shipping, manufacturing, and financial center as well.

The rise of New York City had begun some 50 years before with the building of the Erie Canal, an artificial waterway stretching all the way from New York Harbor to the Great Lakes, connecting New York City to the agricultural and mineral-rich heartland of America. The canal's greatest champion was New York's governor, DeWitt Clinton, who foresaw that by giving New York City merchants, manufacturers, and shippers access to distant goods and markets, the canal would enable the city to become "the greatest commercial emporium in the world." The Erie Canal, Clinton predicted, "will create the greatest inland trade ever witnessed. The most fertile and extensive regions of America will avail themselves of its facilities for a market. All their surplus productions, whether of the soil, the forests, the mines . . . will concentrate in the city of New York for transportation abroad or consumption at home. The city will, in the course of time become the . . . seat of manufacturers [and] the focus of great moneyed operations."

Clinton was right. Within a few years after the canal was built, New York was transformed into a manufacturing and commercial giant. Given the city's ever-increasing growth, its energy and vitality, and its advantageous location, it would, in all probability, have happened anyway. But the canal enabled it to take place much sooner and on a much larger scale than could have previously been imagined. By the 1860s, vast ironworks dominated the landscape along New York's East and Hudson rivers. The waterfronts were filled with barges heaped with New Jersey pig iron and Pennsylvania coal. By 1865 the city housed more than 5,000 manufacturing establishments, large and small, employing more than 125,000 workers.

As hundreds of thousands of manufactured goods poured out of New York's factories and mills, the city's harbor became the busiest port in the world. More than 30,000 ships, carrying a third of all the products exported from the United States and two-thirds of those imported into the nation, passed in and out of New York every year. The hundreds of millions of dollars that both manufacturing and shipping brought into the city led to a proliferation of banks and investment houses that made New York not only the nation's manufacturing and shipping center, but also its financial capital.

And the city kept growing, not only in wealth and excitement, but in national influence as well. "New York is essentially national in interest, position, and pursuits," author James Fenimore Cooper would state. "No one

The Erie Canal became a major artery for transporting passengers as well as freight. By 1845, some 100,000 people were traveling the canal each year.

thinks of the place as belonging to a particular state, but to the United States." Poet Walt Whitman put it this way: "Who does not know," he would write, "that our city is the great place of the western continent - the heart, the brain, the focus, the main spring, the pinnacle, the extremity, the no more beyond of the New World?"

These were not vain boasts. New York City was everything its champions proclaimed it to be. But it was also something else; something far less glamorous, far more disturbing. For the city, with all its accomplishments and all its enticements, had a tremendous problem, one that threatened to destroy all that it had made itself to be.

Even if New York had been built in a spacious area, the challenge of moving the more than one million people who lived or worked in the city or who visited it every day would have been enormous. But New York had been built on the narrow island of Manhattan. Most of its stores, businesses, offices, and other attractions were set in an area only about two miles square. Day by day the streets of New York were becoming so crowded and congested that one of the world's greatest cities was being brought to a standstill. "The throng and rush of traffic in . . . New York is astonishing even for London," wrote a visiting reporter from the *London Times*. "There is a perpetual jam and lock of vehicles for nearly two miles along the chief [thoroughfares]." An editorial in the *New York Evening Post* complained that New York streets were so congested that workers in the city had to spend more than four hours a day getting to and from their jobs.

As early as 1831, city fathers had thought that a solution to the traffic problem had been found. In that year Abraham Brower, a man who had already made his mark in the development of early steamboats and the railroad, created the nation's first urban transportation system in New York when he established an omnibus line designed to carry passengers in buslike vehicles, each pulled by two horses. Brower's line became so popular that by 1835 other lines had been established, and hundreds of often gaily decorated omnibuses (from the Latin word *omni* meaning "all") made their way up and down the streets. Within another ten years, there were so many of the vehicles that newspapers around the country began referring to New York as "the city of omnibuses."

The city's streets were already clogged with hundreds of horse-drawn wagons bringing merchandise to the department stores and shops and carrying freight back and forth from the waterfront area. The scores of private horse-drawn carriages owned by New York's wealthier citizens added to the confusion. Despite their intended purpose of moving people about more easily, the omnibuses made the streets more congested than ever before.

They also made them far more dangerous. "The multitudinous omnibuses," wrote one visitor, "which drive like insane vehicles from morning till night, appear not to pause to take up their passengers, or it is so short a pause you hardly have time to see the stoppage, like the instantaneousness of a flash of lightning. How on earth the people get in and out of them, I do not know: the [driver] surely must sometimes shut a person half in and half out, and cut them in two, but neither he nor they have the time to notice such trifles."

Much of the problem was caused by the rivalry that existed between competing lines. As the omnibuses traveled along the uneven and sometimes cobblestoned streets, their drivers, anxious to gather as many fares as they could, raced against the buses from other lines in order to be the first to reach waiting passengers. Those traveling in the vehicles were jostled about, often banging into one another or being thrown from their seats. Accidents became commonplace, and every year scores of passengers, pedestrians, and drivers of other types of vehicles were injured or even killed. "A ferocious spirit seems to have taken possession of the [omnibus] drivers which defies law and delights in destruction," exclaimed the *New York Herald* in 1859. The *New York Times* put it more simply. "Modern martyrdom," it stated, "may be succinctly defined as riding in a New York omnibus."

As the streets became more and more jam-packed and chaotic, pedestrians found that simply trying to cross the road meant literally risking bodily injury. Businessmen, anxious to get to their meetings and appointments on time, found that, because of the traffic jams, it was virtually impossible to do so. "You cannot accomplish anything in the way of business without devoting a whole day to it," wrote the famed author Mark Twain. "You cannot ride [to where you need to get to] unless you are willing to go in a packed omnibus that labors, and plunges, and struggles along at the rate of three miles in four hours and a half."

It was a frustrating situation, one that was not solved when another form of urban transportation was introduced in New York. In an effort to relieve the problems caused by the omnibuses, transit owners developed the horsecar, a more comfortable and less dangerous way of moving people around. Horsecars looked very much like omnibuses. But instead of being pulled along haphazardly, they were hauled by horses along rails set into the city's streets. Their main benefit was that by traveling along rails on a set route they gave passengers a much smoother ride than the omnibuses.

But more comfortable as they were, the horsecars failed to alleviate the traffic problem. By adding to the number of vehicles that clogged the city's arteries, they actually added significantly to the congestion. And they added to another serious situation as well, one caused by the hundreds of horses that pulled them, the omnibuses, the delivery wagons, and the private carriages through-

Omnibuses and horsecars were intended to solve New York's enormous traffic problems. Instead, they not only created traffic jams of their own but also threatened the lives of the city's pedestrians.

The artist titled this illustration "Pickpockets at work on city railroad cars," illustrating yet another problem with these overcrowded vehicles.

out the city. Every year just one of these horses left as much as ten pounds of manure on the streets every day. Not only did this make crossing the streets—especially for women in their long skirts—a horrendous experience, but the tons of insect-breeding manure placed the health of every resident and every visitor to New York in jeopardy.

And if all this was not enough, there was yet another problem—the incredible amount of almost deafening noise caused by the incessant clamor of the iron-shod hooves and wheels of the horse-drawn traffic, the continual loud gongs of the omnibuses and horsecars, and the constant shrieks and cries from the drivers of the various vehicles. "Under maximum traffic conditions," one writer observed, "a lion's roar would have difficulty making itself heard on the streets of New York." It was no small problem, and it was felt most acutely by those who either lived or worked in the city. Many New York doctors, in fact, attributed the disproportionate number of "nervous diseases" suffered by New Yorkers to the unrelenting noise caused by horse-drawn traffic.

Every one of New York's streets was filled with noise, covered in manure, and clogged with traffic. But it was on Broadway that these conditions were most in evidence. With its block after block of elegant stores, shops, restaurants, and hotels, Broadway was New York's most important thoroughfare. It was also its greatest traffic nightmare, evidenced by the fact that on an average weekday some 15,000 vehicles passed by St. Paul's, the largest church on the street.

"Pack the traffic of the [busiest streets in London into one boulevard] and still you will not have an idea of the crush in Broadway," an English-woman wrote home. "There are streams of scarlet and yellow omnibuses racing in the more open parts, and locking each other's wheels and horses' hoofs. There are loaded stages hastening to and from the huge hotels—carts and wagons laden with merchandise—wheels are locked, horses tumble down, and persons pressed for time are distracted. Occasionally the whole traffic of the street comes to a deadlock. . . . " No wonder that in a letter to his hometown newspaper one visitor wrote, "Shall I describe Broadway to you? It is bedlam on wheels."

Clearly something had to be done to break the logjam that was threatening to choke New York City to death. In 1864, the *New York Herald* stated the situation most precisely. "Something more than horsecars and omnibuses is needed to supply the popular demand for city conveyance," the paper proclaimed. "It must be evident to everybody that neither the cars [n]or the omnibuses supply accommodations enough for the public, and such accommodations as they do supply are not of the right sort."

ENTER ALFRED BEACH

ONE OF THOSE MOST CONVINCED THAT DRAMATIC CHANGE HAD TO TAKE PLACE
if New York City was to survive was a man named Alfred Ely Beach. Every
day, as he gazed out the window of his Broadway office and looked down upon
the bedlam in the street below, he shook his head in dismay. At night, even
though he lived only a few blocks from his office, it took him almost an hour to
dodge the horses, the vehicles, and the milling throngs and make his way home.
Something, he told himself, had to be done.

Beach was not yet 40 years old, but he had already led a remarkable life.
Born in 1826, his father was the founder and owner of the newspaper the *New
York Sun*. Beach received his schooling first at Monson Academy and then at
Yale and was still in his teens when he went to work for his father at the *Sun*,
where he learned much about the publishing business.

He got along well with his father, but he was an ambitious young man who
wanted an enterprise of his own. In 1846 he discovered that a small weekly
journal called *Scientific American* was having financial difficulties and that its
owner, Rufus Porter, had put it up for sale. Beach contacted Oscar Munn, who
had been his classmate at Monson, and together, for $800, they bought the

*Although he remains
largely unknown today,
Alfred Ely Beach was
one of the nation's most
accomplished and daring
innovators and one of its
greatest visionaries.*

magazine. Beach was only 19 years old!

Rufus Porter, who sold *Scientific American* to Beach, was a brilliant but eccentric man who at different times in his life had been a portrait painter, an inventor, and an editor. Under Porter, *Scientific American* provided its readers with some science and technical news, but most of its space was devoted to poetry, moral and religious teachings, and interesting tidbits from around the country. Beach had very different ideas for his new venture.

Along with owning the *Sun*, Beach's father was an inventor of some note, and even as a child the young Beach had been fascinated by the technological discussions he often overheard between his father and the many fellow inventors who came to their home. Young as he still was, Beach was aware that he had bought *Scientific American* at a magical time in the nation's history. It was one of the main reasons he had bought the magazine. Fueled by an inventive spirit unlike anything the world had ever experienced, American innovators from all walks of life were creating a technological revolution that would change almost every aspect of life in the United States. Every day seemed to bring a new invention, leading to a national belief that almost any problem could be solved, any aspect of life made better, by building the proper machine or device.

There were ample reasons for this growing faith in technology. So much mechanical progress was taking place. One had only to look to the American farm for evidence. In the middle of the 1800s, despite the glamour and excitement of cities like New York, Boston, and Chicago, the United States was still predominately a nation of farms and farmers. Farming had always been backbreaking work, filled with long hours and limited productivity. But now, thanks to technological breakthroughs, machines were beginning to change all that. By the end of the 1870s, farm families, particularly those on the vast American prairie who had once struggled to plow or harvest two acres a day, would be able to plow or harvest more than a hundred. Machinery would make it possible for the same farmer who had been forced to limit his wheat crop to about 7 acres to devote more than 135 acres to the crop.

Inventions would not only make farming far more productive; they were already making the farmers' labor easier as well. "The saucy machine," a Kansas newspaper editor exclaimed, "has driven the scythe from the field . . . and the principal work of harvest now is to drive the horse [pulling the machinery] about the field a few times and lo! the harvest is gathered."

The farm machinery that revolutionized American agriculture became one of the great symbols of the Age of Invention.

Beach was aware that it was not only on the farm that technology was bringing about extraordinary change. Throughout the country people were benefiting enormously from Samuel F. B. Morse's invention of the telegraph and the ever-increasing development of a nationwide telegraph system. "Every day affords instances of the advantages our businessmen derive from the use of the telegraph," the *Commercial Review of the South and West* magazine would proclaim. "Operations are made in one day with its aid which could not have been done in two to four weeks by mail."

In 1846, the same year that Beach purchased *Scientific American*, another major breakthrough was made when Elias Howe introduced the world's first sewing machine. Not only did his invention make the age-old task of sewing much easier for people everywhere, but within a few years the sewing machine would revolutionize the garment industry, making clothing more plentiful and more affordable than ever before.

Perhaps most obvious of all were the changes in transportation that had already been brought about by technological developments. The harnessing of steam had led to transportation-related advancements that had, by the time Beach took over *Scientific American*, led to a revolution all its own. "What is this [steam-driven transportation] going to lead to?" the *New York Mirror* had asked in 1835. "Till now man has been bound to a single spot like an oyster or a tree . . . Steam [and the technology it will inspire] is going to alter, in a degree far more remarkable than any previous change, the condition of mankind." The editor had good reason for his prediction. By the 1840s, steamboats, steamships, and steam-driven trains were profoundly changing the way that people moved about.

It was only the beginning. Within a short time, people in all corners of the nation would be given the means to talk directly to one another with an invention called the telephone. Thanks to another invention, the darkness of night would be set aglow. Young as he was, Beach saw an important place for himself in this bold new world. His magazine, he told himself, would be nothing less than the voice of technological change. In the very first issue of *Scientific American* published under his ownership, he announced that the magazine would no longer publish poetry or religious or moral teachings or national trivia. Instead, he declared, it would focus totally on technology and science. An important feature of the magazine would be regular columns devoted to the latest news on new inventions and patent applications.

This illustration in Beach's *Scientific American* showed the drawing that accompanied an inventor's application for a patent for an infantry shield.

Under Beach's initial vision and guidance, *Scientific American* would grow to become one of the nation's most respected and influential magazines, a unique figure in the world of journalism. It would become nothing less than the bible of technical and scientific information. Under Beach, its greatest impact would be in the field of invention, particularly the acquisition of patents. Between 1846 and 1888, the number of patent applications by American innovators rose from 600 to 20,000. It was an astonishing rise, inspired in no small measure by the information published in each issue of *Scientific American*.

Given the magazine's immediate impact, it was not surprising that Beach soon found himself besieged by questions from inventors anxious for help in applying for and securing patents of their own. Many of these inventors put their questions into writing and sent them to Beach at *Scientific American*. Scores of others descended upon the magazine; many of them indicated that they were willing to pay a goodly sum if Beach would personally guide them in securing the type of patent they wanted.

It did not take Beach long to turn this into another business opportunity.

Among the many illustrations in *Scientific American* showing early attempts at manned flight was this one, titled "Ayre's new aerial machine."

Within months of launching his magazine, he, along with Munn, formed the Scientific American Patent Agency, announcing in the magazine that its purpose would be to represent inventors by seeing to it that their patent applications were composed in the most effective manner possible. The new company also pledged that it would monitor the progress of each application once it reached the U.S. Patent Office in Washington.

It was an unprecedented type of business. Never before had there been an agency dedicated to serving inventors in such a way. And it was an immediate and enormous success. So many innovators brought or sent models and descriptions of their inventions to the agency that Beach found himself traveling to Washington every two weeks to personally check up on the progress of his clients' applications. By 1855, the agency had so many clients that Beach and Munn opened up a branch office in Washington, directly across the street from the patent office. Soon other branch offices were established. By the late 1850s, the agency was filing over 3,000 patents a year. By 1860, over one-third of all patents awarded to inventors in the United States had been initially submitted by the Scientific American Patent Agency.

The benefits that Beach derived from the years in which he devoted so much time to the agency went beyond the significant financial rewards the business brought him. Many of the experiences he shared with certain of his clients brought him deep personal satisfaction as well. There was, for example, the day in 1852 on which a plain-looking itinerant cabinetmaker from Pittsfield, Massachusetts, Allen Wilson, appeared unannounced in his offices. After introducing himself, Wilson carefully untied a handkerchief in which were wrapped two small models—one for an improved sewing machine, the other for a rotary engine. He then stated that he could not afford to apply for patents on both inventions and asked Beach for advice on which project he should pursue. With Beach's help, Wilson settled on the sewing machine, which was a vast improvement over Elias Howe's initial invention. Wilson eventually got his patent, and then, with the aid of investors, set up a sewing machine company in Connecticut that became enormously successful. By 1858, the once-poor Wilson, who had come to Beach with his inventions wrapped in a handkerchief, was enjoying life in one of the most beautiful mansions in all of New England.

Most memorable of all for Beach was the day that another young inventor, also without an appointment, appeared at *Scientific American* and without formalities set a small machine on Beach's desk. The inventor stated that he often walked three miles to get his copy of the magazine and that his name was Thomas Edison. Before Beach could reply, he then turned a crank on the machine, and to the astonishment of Beach and several editors who were in

During his amazing career, Thomas Edison, who first demonstrated his phonograph to Alfred Beach, was awarded an astounding 1,093 U.S. patents as well as many others in England, France, and Germany.

the room, the machine said, "Good morning, How do you do? How do you like the talking box?" What the astounded Beach and his editors were being treated to was the first public demonstration of what Edison called the phonograph, among the earliest of what would be hundreds of creations that would eventually earn Thomas Edison his place as the most famous of all inventors.

Beach's unrelenting activities in establishing both *Scientific American* and the world's most successful patent agency would have taxed the physical and mental strength of even the most inexhaustible individuals, but he was a man who seemed to have no limits to his energy. Only two years after he purchased *Scientific American*, his father, impressed with the way Beach had so quickly transformed the once-failing magazine into an important and profitable publication, turned over ownership of the *New York Sun* to him. Somehow, Beach would find the time to make the *Sun* even more successful than it had been when he acquired it.

But even with all these accomplishments, Beach managed to involve himself in yet another endeavor. It was only natural. How could a mechanically talented person who was so taken with technology and inventions, a person continually surrounded by inventors and so immersed in patents, not be inspired to become an inventor himself? He couldn't. And as an inventor, as in everything else he undertook, Beach made his mark.

Among the tens of thousands of patents filed by the Scientific American Patent Agency were more than a score submitted on behalf of Beach himself.

The typewriter, which revolutionized the world of work, was perfected by Christopher Sholes in 1867. But it was Alfred Beach's earlier innovation that paved the way for Sholes's achievement.

Among them was his invention of the world's first cable railway, a system in which passenger-carrying cars were moved along by cables buried in the street. Beach would never follow up on the patent he received, but later, when cable railways were constructed in cities such as San Francisco and Chicago, their builders would follow the design invented by Beach.

Beach's most important invention was one that affected people around the world, both in the home and in the office. Among his other qualities, he was a compassionate person, particularly sympathetic to individuals who suffered disabilities such as blindness. Wishing to help sightless people communicate more effectively, he invented a machine with which blind persons, by pressing raised keys on the device, could create printed messages. Other inventors had been trying to create such a machine for sighted people. But it was Beach who solved the technical problems the other innovators kept encountering and who, in the process, invented the forerunner of the typewriter. When adapted for sighted persons, Beach's invention made work in the nation's growing offices far more efficient than ever before. The typewriter would also have a profound effect on the nature of the American workforce, providing employment opportunities for millions of women.

By the time he was still less than 40 years old, Beach had created a publication that had made him one of the most important figures in the age of technology. He had established a patent agency that enabled thousands of inventors to protect their creations from infringement and bring them to market. He had invented a machine that, once perfected, would transform the business world. But with all these accomplishments, he was still dissatisfied.

How could he be content, he asked himself, when the city he loved so much, the place where he had already been so successful, was all but immobilized by traffic? It was ironic, he thought. People were now traveling great distances across the land and up and down the nation's longest waterways with relative ease. But no one had figured out how to move people efficiently about the city. Night after night, Beach pondered the problem until he came up with a plan. And, like everything he set his mind to, he intended to make it work.

"LIKE A SAIL-BOAT BEFORE THE WIND"

ACTUALLY, BEACH HAD TWO PLANS FOR SOLVING NEW YORK'S HORSE-DRAWN gridlock. One was to build an elevated railroad and to place the traffic high above the streets. But, after giving serious consideration to this idea, he concluded it was not the right solution. An elevated railroad, he came to realize, would only add to the already deafening noise of the city. It would also make the streets beneath it dark and dismal, diminishing the quality of life in entire neighborhoods. And, he decided, it would never be able to carry the number of passengers it would take to truly solve the city's traffic problem.

Increasingly, he came to the conclusion that the only answer was to build a subway—an underground railway that would transport people beneath the city, entirely away from all the street congestion. It was, he knew, a formidable task. Building a subway meant constructing a tunnel and, even more challenging, finding an efficient means of moving passenger cars through it.

Beach was well aware of the London subway that had been built in 1863 and had already carried millions of passengers. But he also knew that there were serious problems connected to that underground railway.

The passenger cars in the London subway were pulled by steam locomotives

Londoners enjoy a stroll through one of the city's tunnels. Before Alfred Beach, however, tunnel building in America was practically an unknown art.

that burned a low grade of coal. They were terribly noisy and, more serious, gave off huge showers of sparks that sometimes rained down upon passengers and train crews alike. Worse yet, the locomotives also belched billows of smoke that clogged passengers' lungs and large amounts of noxious fumes that threatened to poison them. Reports in the London newspapers were filled with accounts of passengers' complaints of "suffocating air," "dreadful smells," "headaches," and "sulphurous taste on the palate." Several London subway riders had become

Thomas Rammell's pneumatic demonstration tube. Rammell constructed it in a way to demonstrate that the car could be successfully propelled around curves.

seriously ill, and more than one had died from the poisonous fumes.

No, thought Beach, locomotives were definitely not the answer to powering his subway. Some other method, totally clean, totally safe, had to be devised. The more he thought about it, the more he realized that the answer was right in front of him. After all, he had been the one who had perfected the pneumatic tube, which allowed small objects to be propelled through a capsule by the force of air. Why not, he thought, use the clean, extraordinarily powerful force of air to power his subway?

Beach not only knew a lot about pneumatics, but also had spent much time studying early, primitive attempts to create pneumatic railways for carrying mail and small parcels. The first of these had been constructed in 1861 by engineer Thomas Rammell, who built a demonstration tube aboveground in the Battersea section of London. In 1863, Rammell and his partner J. Latimer Clark received a charter from the British Postal Service for an underground pneumatic mail delivery service. Rammell and Clark constructed an underground pneumatic tube four feet in diameter and for three years delivered mail and packages, including loads that weighed up to four tons, over a short distance between a London suburb and a district post office. Unfortunately for Rammell and Clark, the cost of running their service exceeded what they were able to charge for pneumatic mail delivery, and in 1866 their company was forced to go out of business. But their story inspired Alfred Beach, particularly when he read about how several thrill seekers had actually snuck aboard Rammell and Clark's cars and had been carried along through the underground tube along with the mail.

Beach derived even greater inspiration from the first pneumatic railway that had been constructed to carry not mail but passengers. It had been built in 1864 on the grounds of England's Crystal Palace Park, the site of the Crystal Palace Exhibition. Beach had fond personal memories of this great industrial exposition. It was there that he had demonstrated his early typewriter and had been awarded a gold medal for his invention.

The Crystal Palace pneumatic railway was built to carry passengers between two of the main gates leading to the exposition. Engineered by the same Thomas Rammell who had designed and built the world's first pneumatic line, it ran for about a quarter of a mile in a brick tunnel ten feet in diameter. Although it was in operation for a relatively short period of time, it made a strong impression, particularly on those seeking advancements in urban transportation. "The entire distance [of the tunnel]," reported *Mechanics Magazine* in 1865, "is transversed in about 50 seconds . . . The motion is of course easy and pleasant, and the ventilation ample, without being in any way excessive . . . We feel tolerably certain that the day is not very distant when metropolitan railway traffic can be conducted on this principle with so much success, as far as popular liking goes, that the locomotive will be unknown on underground lines." It was a prediction with which Alfred Beach was in total agreement. And he was determined that he would be the one to accomplish it.

In his book *Pneumatic Dispatch,* Beach included this drawing of an early demonstration pneumatic railway at Sydenham, England.

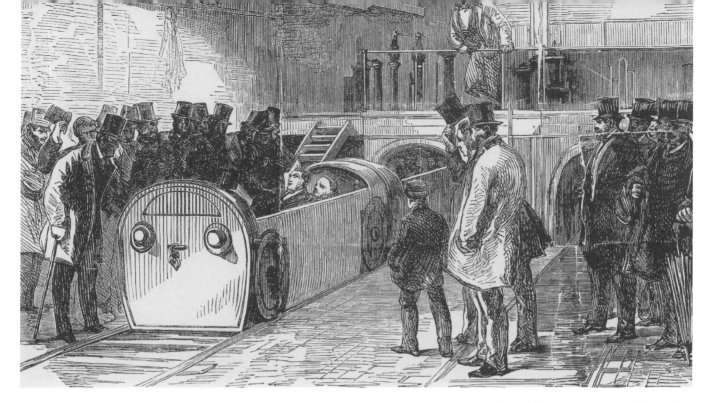

Pictures like this one of another early English pneumatic railway further convinced Alfred Beach that passengers as well as mail could be transported by the power of air.

More than anything else, he knew it would not be easy. It would in fact be more difficult than anything he had ever done. Building a tunnel would in itself present an enormous challenge. Constructing such an underground structure beneath the open Crystal Palace Park was one thing; building a tunnel under the busiest streets of New York City, beneath some of the world's tallest buildings, would be quite another. And there was another problem he would have to face. He knew from having read about the London subway experience that most people of the day had a real fear of descending beneath the earth into what they perceived would be a deep, dark, unnatural environment. Indeed, the London papers regularly carried stories of how the Crystal Palace tunnel had been haunted.

But the greatest challenge of all would be creating a pneumatic system capable of not only propelling passenger cars safely and efficiently through the block-long subway line he intended to build first, but also moving even longer trains of cars over much longer distances once his smaller line was accepted by the public and

Its official name was the
Roots Patent Force Blast
Blower, but Western
Tornado was an
appropriate nickname
for the power source of
Alfred Beach's subway.

he received a license to extend his subway throughout New York. The solution
to this challenge, he concluded, was to equip his subway with machinery that
could deliver the greatest and most controllable force of air possible to move his
cars through the tunnel. This meant acquiring the most powerful fan he could
find to blow the air and a steam engine capable of powering such a fan.

After weeks of investigation, Beach discovered a company in Indiana that
made an extraordinary fanlike machine called a blower. The machine was so
powerful that, when it was combined with an appropriate steam engine, it could
provide a greater force of air than had ever been delivered. Those who made the
blower called it the Western Tornado.

Later, when describing this amazing machine, Beach would write, "This
immense [blower] is by far the largest machine of the kind ever made. It consists
of a great shell of strong iron, twenty-one and a half feet high, sixteen feet long,
and thirteen feet wide, containing two pairs of massive wings, geared together
by cog-wheels, and so arranged that air is drawn in upon one side of the

machine, carried through between the wings, and forced out on the other side . . . This remarkable machine weighs fifty tons, or rather more than a common locomotive engine. The [blower] is to the pneumatic railway what the locomotive is to the ordinary steam railroad. The locomotive supplies the power to draw the car; the [blower] gives . . . force to the air by which the pneumatic car is moved. The [blower] is capable of discharging over one hundred thousand cubic feet of air per minute, a volume equal in bulk to the contents of three ordinary three-story dwelling-houses. The machine makes sixty revolutions per minute . . . " The Western Tornado was indeed a marvel of the age, so massive that when it was eventually delivered to Beach, it was transported from Indiana on a train of five large platform cars.

Acquiring the unique machinery he needed to power his subway moved Beach a giant step toward fulfilling his dream of a pneumatic subway. But he was continually aware that in order to convince all who would be skeptical of his enterprise, he would have to make the subway as appealing and comfortable as possible. He knew, for example, that he would have to design passenger cars that would not only run as smoothly and as silently as possible but also be elegantly appointed.

After hours spent at the drawing board, Beach designed an oval-shaped car about the same size as the omnibuses and horsecars that he hoped his subway would replace. It would be capable of carrying 22 passengers, would run on four wheels, and would have a sturdy airtight door to pneumatically seal it for propulsion. But that was just the beginning. To make the car as lavish as possible, Beach's design called for it to be richly upholstered and to be lit by another marvel of the age. It was the recently invented zircon light, which burned cleaner, purer, and far more brilliantly than the ordinary gaslights of the day.

Lavish as his car design was, it would be the waiting room, Beach decided, that would be the most astounding place in the subway. This room was to be the first place that visitors would encounter as they waited to be transported,

Beach's subway car would offer passengers, accustomed to the bumpy, chaotic rides provided by the omnibuses, the smoothest and most comfortable form of travel they had experienced.

and Beach was determined that it be so elegantly appointed that it would be as beautiful as the finest rooms in New York's best hotels and would leave a magnificent and lasting impression on all who entered it.

Beach's design called for the walls of the waiting room, which he envisioned as being 120 feet long and 14 feet wide, to be covered with paintings by some of the world's greatest artists. Huge chandeliers would hang from the ceiling. Curtains and vases filled with fresh flowers would be strategically placed. There would even be an expensive, tall grandfather clock. The design also called for a special section of the room for ladies, which would contain a grand piano they could play while waiting for the car. Most spectacular of all would be a giant, goldfish-filled cascading fountain that would stand in the center of the room. All this—deep in the bowels of the earth!

It was an audacious plan—from the building of a tunnel the like of which New Yorkers had never encountered to the unprecedented machinery required to provide the unique form of transportation to the elegance of the subway's appointments. But, after completing his plan, Beach was convinced that it would work. To his inventive mind it was, now that he had worked out all the details, quite simple. The blower would drive the car from its starting point to the end of the tunnel "like a sail-boat before the wind." The blower would then reverse the airflow, and the car would be sucked back to its starting point "like soda through a straw." "A tube, car, a revolving fan," Beach would proclaim. "Little more is required."

Given all that would be required, it was, of course, a classic understatement. And Beach knew that as solid as he believed his plan to be, he still had to go a giant step further by physically demonstrating that it could work. His opportunity came in the form of the American Institute Fair, a highly attended industrial exposition that was held each year in New York's mammoth Fourteenth Street Armory.

To introduce the public and the press to the wonders of pneumatic transit and to begin to convince them that a pneumatic subway was the answer to New

York's traffic problem, Beach built a 107-foot-long plywood tube that was 6 feet in diameter. He then designed and constructed a small, open ten-car train to carry passengers along a track inside the tube. Pneumatic power for the train was supplied by a fan ten feet in diameter capable of providing a sufficient blast of air to move the cars to the end of the tube and to bring them back again once the fan was reversed. To demonstrate that pneumatic power could also be used to deliver mail efficiently, Beach constructed a second tube, 24 feet long and 2 feet square, which had a unique attachment that permitted letters to be automatically collected from strategically placed letterboxes and then deposited in the same way at a post office. Once all this was completed, Beach arranged for the tube to be suspended by strong cables from the armory's ceiling.

The American Institute Fair opened on September 12, 1867, but even before it began a *New York Times* reporter, who had been given a sneak preview, wrote of the "startling novelties" that visitors would encounter, among them "a great pneumatic tube, through which the adventurous will be carried north and south

Passengers prepare to ride in Beach's demonstration tube at the American Institute Fair. The October 19, 1867, issue of *Scientific American* reported that with Beach's demonstration the fair "reached its full glory."

according to the fancy or advice of their physicians." Beach himself used the days between the time that the tubes were hung and the fair opened to promote his invention. In one of the articles he published in *Scientific American,* he described his transportation system as "swift as Areolas (the god of breezes) and silent as Somnus (the god of sleep and dreams)."

The giant fair ran for six weeks, and throughout that entire time Beach's pneumatic model was hailed as its most spectacular attraction. More than 170,000 stunned visitors gawked, marveled, and then rode back and forth in the cars, which were kept in constant motion. All the while Beach kept up his unabashed promotion of his creation. "The most novel and attractive feature of the exhibition is by general consent conceded to be the Pneumatic Railway," he wrote, "and everyone visiting the Fair seems to consider himself specially called upon to visit, and, after actual experience, to pronounce his verdict upon this mode of traveling."

The verdicts were unanimously glowing. The press and public alike pronounced the Pneumatic Railway an enormous success. Most important to Beach were the newspaper articles that predicted how such a system would transform New York from a transportation nightmare to a transit miracle. "It is . . . estimated," stated the *Times,* "that passengers by a through city tube could be carried from City Hall to Madison-Square in five minutes, to Harlem and Manhattanville in fourteen minutes, to Washington Heights in twenty minutes, and by sub-river to Jersey City or Hoboken in five minutes . . . " To cap off his triumph, the officials of the American Institute ended the fair by awarding Beach both of its top prizes, one for the exhibition of the Pneumatic Railway, the other for the Postal Dispatch.

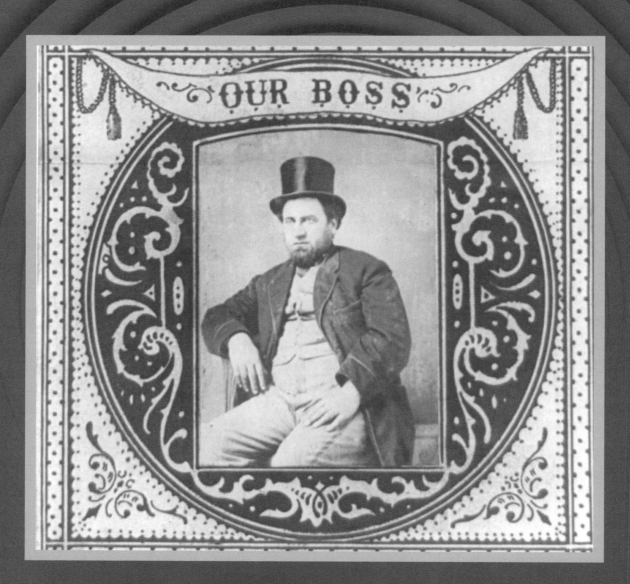

OVERCOMING BOSS TWEED

ALFRED BEACH WAS NOT ONLY A PROVEN INNOVATOR AND ONE OF THE greatest visionaries of his time; he was also a practical and politically savvy man. He was aware that it was one thing to build a model subway by constructing a plywood tube and having it hung from the ceiling of an armory and quite another to bore a tunnel under one of the busiest streets in the world. He also knew that before he could dig one shovelful of dirt, he had to get a charter to build his subway from city and state officials. More than anything else, that meant getting approval from the most powerful man in New York, a man so powerful that nothing got done in the city without his consent. His name was William Marcy Tweed. Most people called him Boss, and he was not only the most powerful person in New York but also the most corrupt politician that city—or any other American city—had ever seen.

Before his legendary career was over, millions of words would be written about the man who many of his time would regard as a 19th century Robin Hood, while others would describe him as the ultimate unscrupulous, money-grasping, influence-peddling politician. "He was a natural politician, a gregarious, good-natured backslapper who, by handing out jobs and charity earned the love

This label from a can of tobacco shows William Marcy Tweed early in his rise to political power. Tweed would become Alfred Beach's greatest obstacle to giving New York its first subway.

and loyalty of [common people], especially the [millions] of Irish immigrants," the *New York Times* would write. Another newspaper would describe him as "a healthy boon companion, a lover of his friends, and generous to the 'boys.'" And an English visitor to New York would declare, "He had an abounding vitality, plenty of humor, though of a coarse kind, and a jovial swaggering way."

Those were among the kindest words written about him. But others assessed him much differently. Long after Tweed had died, author E. L. Doctorow, responding to those who emphasized Tweed's fun-loving ways and generosity to those whose votes he bought, would write, "I know what you people . . . think; you look back on Boss Tweed with affection as a wonderful fraud, a legendary scoundrel of old New York. But what he accomplished was murderous in the very modern sense of the term, manifestly murderous. Those he couldn't bribe, he bullied . . . he bought the drinks and paid for the dinners, but in the odd moment when there was no hand to shake or toast to give, the eye went dead and you saw the soul of a savage."

Physically, Tweed was an unforgettable character. He was about six feet tall and, for most of his adult life, weighed over 320 pounds. He had a large bald head and sported a red beard. What struck most people on first meeting him were his bright blue eyes, which seemed to twinkle when he found something amusing. But when he was angry these same eyes turned to cold steel, as they did on the occasion when he actually stared down a person holding a knife to his huge stomach, causing the man to drop the weapon and flee. What was perhaps most noticeable about him was his enormous appetite. Descriptions of some of the gargantuan meals he ate border on the unbelievable. Blessed with limitless energy, he was a consummate workaholic.

This photograph was taken shortly after Boss Tweed became a member of the U.S. House of Representatives, one of the many political posts he used to enrich himself.

For years, Boss Tweed's abuse of power escaped the attention of most of the general public. Eventually, however, his misdeeds would catch up with him.

Tweed was born in 1823 on New York's Lower East Side. He floundered along for his first 21 years, earning a reputation as both a bully and a brawler. At the age of 26, however, his life changed when he formed his own volunteer fire brigade. At the time, these fire companies were as much social and political clubs as they were protectors of the public. Through the force of his personality and his ever-growing ambitions, he ingratiated himself with the Irish, German, and other immigrants and decided that he had a real future in politics.

He began by running for and winning a seat on the New York Board of Aldermen, a post that launched him into a meteoric political career. By handing out money and gifts and delivering favors to those who voted for him, he was elected or appointed to a staggering number of positions, including congressman, state senator, president of the county board of commissioners, New York City street commissioner, and New York City commissioner of public works. They were all powerful positions, each presenting him the opportunity to step outside the law and enrich himself.

This illustration in *Harper's Weekly* shows Tammany Hall workers in front of a voting place. They are threatening violence to those who would dare to vote against Tammany Hall candidates.

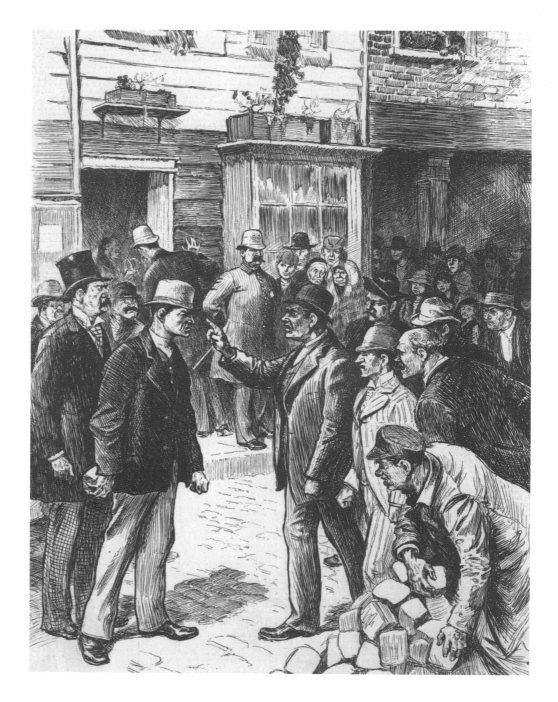

His greatest triumph came in 1858 when he got himself elected head of a political organization known as Tammany Hall. By surrounding himself with equally dishonest men, he soon turned Tammany Hall into the nation's most corrupt political machine.

Under Tweed's leadership, bribery became Tammany Hall's trademark. Through payoffs, Tweed and his cronies controlled governors, mayors, and newspaper editors. They paid dishonest judges to make rulings in their favor. They provided reductions in taxes to rich people who paid them back in bribes. They rigged elections to assure that city officials would let them do whatever they pleased. And they sold political appointments to those who promised to let them carry on as they pleased.

Among the most outrageous of Tammany Hall's activities was their involvement in the building of a new county courthouse located behind New York City Hall. Authorization for its construction had been granted in 1858 with $250,000 set aside for the project. Construction under Commissioner Tweed's oversight began in 1862, but due to delays caused by Tweed's and his cronies' maneuvers to steal as much money from the project as they could, the building was not completed until ten years later. By that time the inflated fees that Tweed paid to builders and suppliers in return for kickbacks resulted in a final cost to the city and its taxpayers of more than 12 million dollars. Even with the delays and kickbacks, construction of the courthouse should have cost no more than 3 million. Tweed and his fellow rogues walked away with the remaining 9 million dollars.

Almost all of Tammany Hall's officials took part in these illicit activities, but the most outrageous of them all were carried out by Tweed himself. As an alderman, he was one of those responsible for selecting which run-down areas were to be torn down and scheduled for development. Knowing that these places would then become extremely valuable, he purchased those areas marked for improvement and made himself a fortune. His position as commissioner of public works gave him a special opportunity to enrich himself by awarding contracts only to builders who would agree to pay him a hefty kickback for every job. Some of the contracts Tweed awarded were for work that was never done. That was fine with him as long as he got his payment. When he was elected to the New York City Board of Education, he further padded his bankroll by selling appointments to teachers and by letting publishers know that their textbooks would only be purchased for the city's schools if the publishers paid him a bribe.

As if all this corruption and money grabbing were not enough, the insatiable Tweed found yet another avenue for enriching himself. Increasingly, he used his power to get himself elected to the boards of directors of some of the nation's largest businesses and business enterprises. Chief among these were the Erie Railroad, whose officials paid Tweed more than $650,000 (more than 10 million dollars today) for using his influence to assure that laws favorable to the railroad were passed. Similarly, when the enormous Brooklyn Bridge was about to be built, Tweed made it crystal clear that construction would not be allowed to begin until he was put on the bridge company's board and paid a huge sum.

All told, it is estimated that during his heyday, Tweed stole more than $200,000 (more than 3 million dollars today). It was enough to make him one of the richest men in New York. By the time Alfred Beach was ready to build his subway, Boss Tweed was the third-largest landowner in the city. Among his many holdings was one of New York's grandest hotels and one of its largest printing houses, a firm that reaped huge profits from the inflated contracts it received from Tweed-influenced city agencies.

It all resulted in enormous ill-gotten wealth, which Tweed openly flaunted. He had two steam yachts, a private railway car, and several homes, including a New York City mansion and a lavish country estate in Connecticut. Among his favorite possessions was a huge diamond pin that he wore every day on his shirtfront. The pin alone was worth more

Much of Tammany Hall's success was due to the way it distributed favors to newcomers to America. Here party workers recruit newly arrived immigrants.

than $300,000 in today's currency.

Aside from trying to make himself as rich as he possibly could, Tweed had even greater ambitions. His fondest dream was to raise his power to the national level by using his influence to make one of his cronies president of the United States, another of his henchmen governor of New York, and through the power that gave them, get himself elected to the United States Senate. Even he could not estimate how much money he would be able to steal and how much power he would wield from that lofty position.

47

This illustration from Beach's book *Pneumatic Dispatch* was intended to show how his proposed subway would efficiently transport large packages.

What did this all mean to Alfred Beach? For one thing, he knew that Tweed would never allow him to build his subway unless Beach agreed to pay him a significant share of whatever profits the subway collected in fares.

A proud and honest man, Beach knew that he could never permit himself to agree to such a bribe. Equally important, Beach was aware that among the scores of businesses that paid Tweed a hefty kickback in order to carry out their operations were the various omnibus and horsecar companies. Tweed, he realized, would never approve the building of an underground passenger-carrying transit system that, if successful, would probably put

According to Beach's plan, letters would be conveniently delivered underground to collection boxes attached to lampposts located throughout the city.

the omnibus and horsecar companies out of business.

Beach had been nothing short of ingenious in creating a bold and unprecedented plan for solving New York's transportation problem. Now, he realized, he had to be equally bold and inventive in finding a way to make sure that Boss Tweed would not destroy his dream before he could even begin to turn it into reality. After many sleepless nights considering one course of action after another, he came up with a daring idea. Knowing that Tweed would block any attempt to build a passenger-carrying subway, he decided that he would apply for a charter calling for a subway designed solely for the underground delivery of mail and small packages, not people. Once he had his charter in hand, he would build his passenger subway.

When this plan was formulated, Beach formed what he called the Beach Pneumatic Dispatch. He then applied to the New York state legislature for the right to build two small underground tubes through which mail and packages could be delivered pneumatically. When Tweed reviewed the application he saw no challenge to his many interests, and without his interference the legislature granted Beach a 50-year charter to build his two tubes under Broadway. But Beach was not done with his maneuverings. With this license in hand, he reapplied to the legislature for an amendment to his charter asking for the right to build a larger single tube which, he stated, would be more efficient for transporting mail. Unaware that his purpose in doing so was to have a tube large enough to carry passengers, the unsuspecting lawmakers granted Beach the amendment.

He was ready to begin. But in order to do so he would have to do something that no one in the world had ever done. Not only would he have to build a subway that would so impress city and state officials, the public, and the press that they would forgive his deception, but he would have to do it without anyone finding out about it until it was completed. The nation's first subway was about to be built in secret!

BUILDING THE SUBWAY

A SUBWAY BUILT IN SECRET—UNDER THE BUSIEST STREET IN ONE OF THE BUSIEST cities in the world. One can hardly imagine a more daunting or improbable task. But Beach had planned well, and he was confident he could pull it off.

The challenges were enormous. For one, Beach knew that in order to have the least chance of detection, all of the work would have to be done at night after the omnibuses and horsecars stopped running and most of the Broadway foot traffic had ceased. He also knew that he had to find a building located above where a portion of his tunnel was to be dug. The structure had to have a basement that the workers could use as a base of operations.

Such a basement was, in fact, essential to keeping the subway's construction a secret. The digging of the tunnel would result in the accumulation of tons of dirt and sand that had to be removed from the site. Where was it all to be stored? How could it be carted away without detection? Beach's solution was simple and typically daring. The dirt and sand would be stored in whatever basement he could find. Then it would be regularly carted away under the cover of darkness in wagons with muffled wheels.

A view of Broadway in 1870. The tall building with an awning on the left is Devlin's Clothing Store, under which Beach began constructing his subway.

After checking out all the buildings on the side of Broadway under which the tunnel was to be built, Beach found what he wanted. It was Devlin's Clothing Store—and it came with a huge bonus. It had not one level of basement, but two, plus another large underground room that extended from the lower basement and served as the store's vault. It was ideal for Beach's purposes and, after negotiating with the store's owners, he was able to secure a five-year lease for all the underground space.

It was a big step forward, but one giant challenge remained. Tunneling in the United States was practically an unknown endeavor. Very few had ever been dug. No effective machinery to do so had been developed. How, then, would the tunnel be dug?

There was only one answer. Beach would have to create a tunnel-digging machine. And, as he had done with his typewriter, his cable car system design, and his pneumatic tube, he invented a device that would change forever the way yet another task was carried out.

He called his tunnel digger a hydraulic shield. Cylindrical and open at both ends, it looked like an open-ended barrel. Attached to it were 18 steel bars that were driven against the portion of the tunnel that had already been completed by the force of water from a hand pump within the shield. The water from the pump exerted a pressure of some 126 tons, which not only kept the hydraulic shield stable but also drove the machine forward 16 inches at a time. This enabled the extremely sharp front edge of the device to cut through the earth with relative ease. One of the machine's most important features was the metal hood above the device that extended some three feet back and protected workers inside the shield from cave-ins.

One worker operated the water pump. Once a 16-inch section of earth had been dug, other workers put the loosened soil into wheelbarrows and wheeled it through the completed portion of the tunnel into Devlin's basement, where it remained until it was carted away. At the same time, other workers, standing

Devlin's Clothing Store, in whose basement Beach had the dirt removed from his tunnel, was one of the largest retailers of men's, women's, and children's clothing in the nation.

This illustration, which appeared in *Frank Leslie's Illustrated Newspaper* on February 19, 1870, showed how workmen checked the alignment of Alfred Beach's tunnel at every stage of its construction.

under the protection of the hood, bricked in the walls of the portion of the tunnel that had just been dug. Awkward as it looked, the hydraulic shield was extremely flexible and could move left or right, up or down. With it, some eight feet of the tunnel was dug every night. Without it, the subway would never have been completed.

It also never would have been finished if Beach had not been willing to involve himself personally in every aspect of the project. Night after night, he went down into the tunnel. He encouraged the workers, dealt with whatever problems they encountered, and revised his plan wherever necessary. But he had no experience in building tunnels, and he was wise enough to know that he needed someone who did. Fortunately, he was able to hire the foremost, and perhaps only, tunneling expert living in America to serve as the chief engineer of the project. His name was John Dixon, and he was an Englishman familiar with tunnels that had been constructed in Great Britain, including the London subway.

It was a wise choice. Dixon was not only highly organized but was also particularly knowledgeable about the most effective way of supporting a tunnel with iron plates and steel arches in order to make it as safe and secure as possible. He had first caught Beach's attention at the American Institute Fair where Beach had won a gold medal for his pneumatic subway model. At the same fair, Dixon had also been awarded a gold medal for his exhibition of "Cast Iron Plates for Underground Railways."

Among Dixon's most important innovations for fortifying a tunnel was the employment of steel arches placed at strategic points along the tunnel's route. Along with the steel plates that would line the sides of the structure, these arches would guarantee the tunnel's strength. In an article he wrote for *Scientific American*, Beach described the advantages of using Dixon's method for fortifying his subway. "In applying Mr. Dixon's method to underground railways . . ." he wrote, "a foundation of stone is . . . placed, to which the side [iron] plates are bolted, and [then] plates forming an arch are . . . placed on a movable framework and bolted to each other . . . The ease with which the parts are put together, their comparative cheapness of cost, the facility with which they may be handled and transported to the place required, render it incomparably superior to every other method of tubing hitherto employed . . . In the construction of tunnels where [workers must dig] through a loose soil, the advantages of arches [to further strengthen the tunnel are unsurpassed]."

By inventing the hydraulic shield and by employing John Dixon and adopting his method of fortifying a tunnel, Beach had done what he could to assure that the subway would be constructed in the best way possible. But it was still an extremely difficult and dangerous task.

For all those involved, working secretly more than 21 feet underground was frightening, to say the least. The zircon lighting for the tunnel could not be installed until the tunnel was completed, and the subterranean darkness, lit only by flickering lanterns, added to the laborers' uneasiness. Even though the work was carried out after the omnibuses and horsecars stopped running, there was still late-night horse traffic on Broadway, and hoofbeats could distinctly be heard overhead. Beach, in particular, worried that a galloping horseman would crash through the tunnel's ceiling, not only injuring workmen but also exposing the project. The claustrophobic conditions, the dim lighting, the stuffy air, and the very real fear of being killed proved too much for a number of the workers, who put down their tools and quit.

But, urged on by Beach and his son Fred, who served as foreman of the digging crews, the work continued. Night after night, eight feet or more of soil was dug and carted away and eight feet of brick was cemented onto the tunnel's walls. The sight of the hydraulic shield moving ever forward, and the sound of picks and shovels digging into the loosened earth were music to Beach's ears. Then, suddenly, he heard a new and alarming sound. The hydraulic shield had run into a solid stone wall.

For the first time since digging had begun, all work came to a halt. What was this stone wall, everyone wondered. (Later it was revealed that it was the large

In this drawing, published in the February 19, 1870, issue of *Frank Leslie's Illustrated Newspaper*, the artist focused on revealing both the iron plates that John Dixon had invented and the way in which the tracks were laid.

foundation of an old Dutch fort, built in the colonial period by people from the Netherlands who had been the first to settle New York). More important, could it be removed safely?

It was the most serious problem that Beach had yet encountered. If the wall could not be removed, he would probably have to abandon the project. But attempting to take down the wall might well cause the street above to collapse upon them, killing them all. He had an agonizing decision to make, but he made it. "Remove it," he ordered, "stone by stone."

For the next several nights, workmen painstakingly chipped away at the wall and took it apart one stone at a time. All the while, Beach stared at the ceiling hoping upon hope that it would hold firm. Fortunately it did, and as soon as the last stone was removed, the digging resumed.

Amazingly, the fact that Beach and his workers were building a passenger subway was all kept secret. Those, particularly newspaper reporters, who could not help but notice that something was going on under Broadway believed that it was the digging of a small railway for delivering mail. That, after all, was what Beach had told the legislature he was going to do. But with so much activity taking place, it was impossible not to arouse curiosity. This was particularly true on the day that the huge blower and fan were delivered and had to be

placed on the corner of Broadway and Warren before being laboriously lowered into the subway. It was a time when all those involved in the project had to be particularly tight-lipped.

"Warren St., as stated yesterday," reported the *New York Times*, "is strewn with huge pieces of machinery. Laborers are tugging at them, all the while looking as wise as owls, but dumb as sphinxes . . . All means of communicating with [the workmen] are cut off or so guarded that one cannot [get a word out of them]."

Another anxious moment took place when it was noticed that a section of the pavement on Broadway had become slightly depressed. Beach knew that this had been caused by something other than the tunnel excavation, but he was concerned that officials would want to come down into the tunnel to make sure that the digging had not caused the problem. Once in the tunnel, they would, of course, discover Beach's secret. He solved this problem by speaking directly with the press and convincing them that the depression in the street had nothing to do with his project.

"Something has been said in regard to the caving-in of the surface of the east side of Broadway above the Pneumatic tube," wrote the *New York Times*. "There is certainly a flattening of the surface of the Broadway pavement near Warren street, but whether this is due to the underground excavations or to the imperfect manner which the pavement was laid is questionable. The [Pneumatic] company declare that . . . the caving-in of the street is all nonsense."

Fortunately, city officials chose to believe that the problem had been caused by faulty paving and decided not to make a premature inspection of Beach's "mail-delivery system." The secret was still intact. The work went on without detection, and soon the digging of the tunnel was nearly finished. Remarkably, it had taken only 58 nights.

There was still much work to be done. All the lighting needed to be installed. The walls of the tunnel needed to be painted white. Track had to be laid down and the subway car placed upon it. The installation of the blower and the fan had to be completed. And all the elegant trappings of the waiting room had to be put in place. But the greatest challenge, constructing the first real underground tunnel in America, had been met.

Beach had done it. And despite all the obstacles he had faced, he had done it brilliantly. As one transit authority would later proclaim, "The marvel, the absolute marvel is that they were able to construct this thing and it wasn't a half-baked thing; it was a magnificent piece of construction. [Beach] was a transportation undercover agent, battling against the [forces] of Tweed and his other Tammany cronies . . . It was a melodrama, but he pulled it off."

Aware that theirs was an engineering feat unprecedented in America, one that depended on gaining approval from the public, the press, and New York politicians, Beach and John Dixon monitored the subway's progress every step of the way.

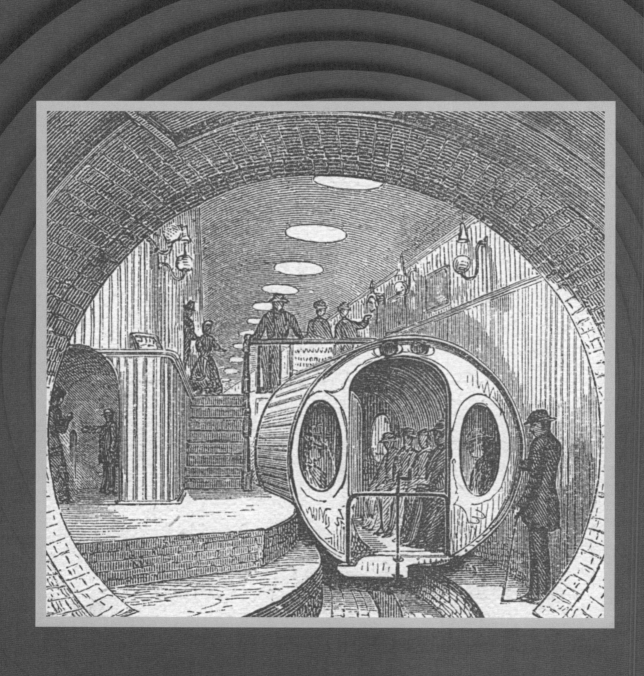

THE SUBWAY REVEALED

A rare glimpse of
the waiting station,
seemingly the only one
ever drawn, showing
the paintings that hung
on the wall, but not the
chandelier, the fountain,
or the grand piano.

BY THE END OF THE FIRST WEEK OF JANUARY 1870, BEACH AND THE WORKMEN
were well on their way to completing the subway. But then something that
Alfred Beach had not counted upon took place. Somehow, a reporter for the
New York Herald got wind of what was really going on underneath Broadway.
Disguising himself as a workman, he entered Devlin's Store, made his way down
into the basement, and saw for himself what had been taking place there. Beach
should probably not have been surprised. In many ways it was remarkable that
so much activity, involving so many workers, could have been carried out for so
long without being discovered.

By the second week in January both the *Herald* and the *New York Tribune* ran
huge stories revealing Beach's secret to the world. "The oldest inhabitant, who
remembers [New York] when tunnels under Broadway were never thought of, will
reflect upon this exploit with wonder and thanks . . . " exclaimed the *Tribune*.
"Thus far little has been accomplished for the imagination or the senses by the
diggers of the tunnel; but any glimpse of their work just now must be interesting to
all who wish to see the world of New York relieved of its giant swarm."

With news of the passenger subway now out in the open, Alfred Beach

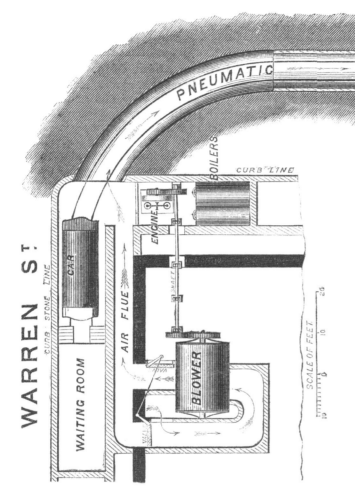

PNEUMATIC CAR TUNNEL

BROADWAY

WARREN ST.

CURB STONE LINE

CAR

WAITING ROOM

AIR FLUE

ENGINE

SHAFT

BOILERS

CURB LINE

BLOWER

SCALE OF FEET

knew that he had to act. Confident that what he had accomplished would so impress city officials that they would overlook his deception in building a passenger railway and would grant him a charter to begin extending the subway throughout New York, he decided to hold a lavish reception and viewing for dignitaries and the press. He would then open the subway to the public.

But he had to make sure that everything was as perfect as he could make it before the press followed up its initial disclosures by clamoring for the subway to be open to view. His first step was to have John Dixon write a letter to all the newspapers explaining the brief delay. "Our original intention," Dixon stated, "was to construct the entire line of tunnel from Warren to Cedar Street, before opening it to inspection, but we have concluded to yield to the strong desire manifested by the Press for earlier examination. We have, therefore stopped work on the tunnel, and are now fitting up the blowing machinery, engines, boilers, waiting rooms, etc, with a view of inviting public inspection . . . Our tunnel commences at the southwest corner of Broadway and Warren Street, curving out to the center of Broadway and continuing down a little below Murray Street . . . The top of the

This detailed diagram of Alfred Beach's subway shows, among other things, the placement of the giant blower, the passenger car, the waiting room, the air flue, and the tunnel.

tunnel comes within twelve feet of the pavement, so that the walls of adjoining buildings can in no way be affected. We should have preferred to keep silent until our work could speak for us; as it is we beg the press to have a little patience, and in three or four weeks at furthest we will cheerfully afford them an opportunity of inspecting our premises and forming their own judgment as to its merits."

By the third week in February, Beach was confident that all the final tasks had been completed and that he was ready to open the subway for all to see. On February 26th he held his giant reception for city and state officeholders and the press. And it was an enormous success.

Given the anticipation that led up to it and the mystery that surrounded it, the subway that had been built in secret was a huge story, and every newspaper in New York featured it prominently. "PROPOSED UNDERGROUND RAILROAD—A FASHIONABLE RECEPTION HELD IN THE BOWELS OF THE EARTH—THE GREAT BORE EXPOSED," read the headline in the *Herald*.

Reporting on the reception, the *New York Times* stated, "The opening was a very pleasant occasion. It was intended especially for dignitaries, legislators, aldermen, scientific men, and members of the press, and scores of them were present. Mr. Beach himself was conspicuous, making his explanations and entertaining visitors like princes. Judge Daly, members of the American Institute, City officials, and many prominent citizens were observed among those who came . . . At nightfall the unique occasion was over, but the 'Transit Company' had made a host of friends and supporters."

Two days later the *Times* reported on a special visit made to the subway by important members of the Railroad Committee of the New York legislature. "The Committee," stated the *Times,* "expressed much astonishment at the magnitude of the enterprise . . . as well as at the extent of the subterranean work already accomplished. They transversed with Mr. Dixon the entire length of the tunnel thus far completed, and made a minute examination of its construction. The ponderous machinery erected at the entrance to the tunnel—to be used as the blowing apparatus for propelling the cars through the tunnel—excited much curiosity and surprise."

It was high praise, but many of the other newspapers were even more effusive. "The problem of tunneling Broadway has been solved," exclaimed the *Evening Mail*. "There is no mistake about it ... the work has been pushed vigorously on by competent workmen, under a thoroughly competent superintendent, whose name is Dixon. May his shadow increase for evermore! ... [Visits to the subway] will be followed by a general hallelujah no sane man doubts ... It is truly most gratifying to see how admirably the affair has been carried out so far."

And the unqualified praise did not stop there. "Different papers [will] give different accounts of the enterprise," the *Sunday Mercury* wrote, "but the opening yesterday must have convinced them all of the powers of human imagination." "A remarkable work, planned and executed in a remarkable manner," stated *Frank Leslie's Illustrated Newspaper*. And, in a statement that may well have been the most gratifying of all to Alfred Beach, the *Herald*, the newspaper whose reporter had first unlocked his secret, boldly proclaimed the reception and viewing to be nothing less than "the opening day of the first underground railway in America."

Altogether, it was greater praise and approval than even Beach could have hoped for. Buoyed by this initial success, he then announced that, on March 1, the subway would be open to the public. For 25 cents a ticket, the proceeds of which would be donated to charity, New Yorkers could not only inspect every aspect of the subway but also experience what, according to Beach, was the future of urban transit in New York: riding underground in a car propelled by air.

Once again, his hopes were bolstered by the press. "Any description of the Pneumatic Railway," exclaimed the *World*, "must necessarily be imperfect; the work must be thoroughly appreciated . . . Everyone should invest a quarter . . . and they will be well repaid for the outlay." If these statements were not enticing enough, yet another article in the *Times* added to the public's desire to view what some who had already seen the subway were now calling Aladdin's

This illustration of one of his proposed stations was typical of the drawings Beach published in *Scientific American* to illustrate the benefits of his subway once it was expanded throughout New York.

Cave. "Certainly," stated the *Times*, "the most novel, if not the most successful enterprise that New York has seen in many a day is the Pneumatic Tunnel under Broadway. A myth, or a humbug, it has been called by everybody who has been excluded from its interior, but hereafter the public can have the opportunity of examining the undertaking and judging of its merits. [When the tunnel was thrown open to official visitors] it must be said that every one of them came away surprised and gratified. Such as expected to find a dismal, cavernous retreat under Broadway, opened their eyes at the elegant reception room, the light, airy tunnel and the general appearance of taste and comfort in all the apartments, and those who entered to pick out some scientific flaw in the project, were

silenced by the completeness of the machinery, the solidity of the work, and the safety of the running apparatus."

Inspired by what they had read, thousands of people thronged to the subway on its opening day. And they were shocked by what they encountered. Even with all that many of them had read in the newspapers, they were astounded by the elegance of the waiting room. Chandeliers? Fountains filled with goldfish? Grand pianos? Fine paintings lining the walls? Here in the bowels of the earth? It was almost beyond belief.

Many of the visitors had come just to see the tunnel. And they were not disappointed. Beach had known from the beginning that one of his biggest challenges would be that of convincing the public that his tunnel would be bright, airy, solid, and, unlike the London subway, free of smoke and fumes. For most of the visitors it took just one walk along the length of the tunnel to see that this subway was both safe and less frightening than they could have imagined.

It was all new; it was all wondrous, and, for most, the greatest experience of all was their first ride on the pneumatic railway. "We took our seats in the pretty car, the gayest company of twenty that ever entered a vehicle," a woman passenger would later write. "The conductor touched a telegraph wire on the wall of the tunnel and before we knew it, so gently was the start, we were in motion, moving from Warren Street down Broadway. In a few moments the conductor opened the door and called out, Murray Street with a business-like air that made us all shout with laughter. The car came to rest in the gentlest possible style, and immediately began to move back to Warren Street where it had no sooner arrived, than in the same gentle and mysterious manner it moved back again to Murray Street; and thus continued to go back and forth for I should think twenty minutes, or until we had all ridden as much as we desired. No visible agency gave motion to the car, and the only way that we inside could tell that we were being moved by atmospheric pressure was by holding our hands against the ventilators over the doors. When these were opened strong currents of pure air came into the car. We could also feel the air current pressing inward at the

A sketch from the
March 12, 1870, issue
of *Harper's Weekly*.

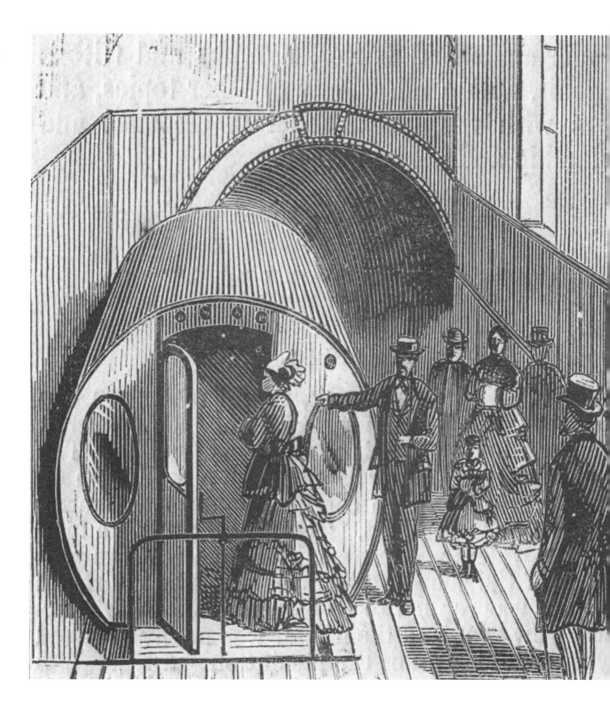

bottom of the door. I need hardly say that the ventilation of the pneumatic car is very perfect and agreeable, presenting a strong contrast to the foul atmosphere of [omnibuses and horsecars]. Our atmospheric ride was most delightful, and our party left the car satisfied by the actual experience that the pneumatic system of traveling is one of the greatest improvements of the day."

Like the woman passenger and her car mates, almost every person who took his or her first "atmospheric ride" found it a marvelous experience. But for some brave and curious souls, there was another experience that was far less serene. These individuals had read about the awesome power of the Western Tornado and were determined to observe it close-up. "After we had had our ride," one of them would later write, "it was only natural of course that we should wish to explore the source from whence came the pneumatic pressure that had so mysteriously carried us along under Broadway. Accordingly, under the guidance of one of the polite officials of the company, provided with lanterns, we entered the air-passage or duct, which opens into the waiting room near the mouth of the tunnel. This passage is fifty or sixty feet long and four and a half feet high. As we went in, we felt a gentle breeze; but after we arrived at the mouth of the great blower, and while we were gazing in wonder at the motions of the gigantic blowing-wings, the engineer put on more steam and increased the speed, so that the blast instantly became a hurricane of frightful power. Hats, bonnets, shawls, handkerchiefs, and every loose thing were snatched away from our hands and swept into the tunnel, while all of us, unable to stand against the tornado hastily retreated from the machine to a corner of the air-box, where we werw. . . sheltered. At this juncture the speed of the [Western Tornado] was reduced, the storm was over, and only a gentle summer's breeze issued from its enormous throat. We retired from the presence of the machine . . . thankful that it did not blow the life out of us."

The Western Tornado had indeed thrown a scare into those who had needed to be convinced of its power. But it was an experience that only added to their assessment that the pneumatic railway was a true marvel. One can only imagine the satisfaction that Alfred Beach derived as he read through such passenger's comments as: "It was like being aboard a fairy ship." "The car floated . . . like a feather gliding on air." "A more agreeable mode of traveling can scarcely be conceived."

Even more important to the man who had spent much of his personal fortune and had staked his future on the project were the statements that predicted the way in which the unique subway would, at last, bring an end to New York's traffic problem and make life better for all its citizens. In their enthusiasm for the subway, some of the comments went a bit overboard. The editor of *Youth's Companion,* for example, envisioned the possibility of the tunnel someday being extended under the ocean all the way to Europe. "So the world goes on," he wrote, "doing more and more wonderful things every day, and who knows but that before you . . . readers are old men and women, you and I may go down [into the subway], and in a twinkling find ourselves in England. Who knows?"

It was a fanciful notion, of course, but above all else Alfred Beach knew that it was time to take advantage of the universal acclaim that had been heaped upon his project by city officials, the press, and the public alike. He now boldly began to push for a charter that would eventually allow him to extend his subway to every corner of New York. "We propose to begin operations on a subway all the way to Central Park," he would state. "When it's finished we should be able to carry 20,000 passengers a day at speeds up to a mile a minute."

Pushing his cause further, he would add, "The days of dusty horsecars and rumbling omnibuses are almost at an end. Snow and dust, heat and cold find no kingdom [in the pneumatic subway]. Warm in winter and cool in summer. . . the weary man or woman who [now] spends hours daily getting to and from business may, when that joyful day of a completed underground comes, allow five minutes for going five miles . . . "

THE END OF TWEED

Commenting on the photographs that were taken once Beach's subway became known, the *New York Evening Post* exclaimed, "Photography has been brought to such perfection that even the bowels of the earth yield to its mysteries."

THE PUBLIC, THE PRESS, AND MOST CITY AND STATE OFFICIALS WERE THRILLED by what Beach had accomplished—but not William "Boss" Tweed. When he read the glowing newspaper accounts of the subway he was at first dumbfounded. Then he became as furious as most of his Tammany Hall cohorts had ever seen him. How could anyone, he fumed, have built a passenger subway without him knowing about it? And right across the street from where he spent so much of his time. More important, how could anyone dare to do such a thing without paying him the appropriate bribe? Well, he thought, he'd soon put an end to Alfred Beach.

Told of Tweed's outrage, Beach had a simple reply. "New York," he stated more emphatically than ever, "needs a subway." One thing he knew for certain: He had to take advantage of the tremendous enthusiasm his subway had generated by applying to the state legislature for a charter allowing him to begin to extend his pneumatic transit system throughout New York. Specifically, his application asked for the right to start by extending the subway all the way to Central Park, a distance of some five miles. In applying for the license, he also stated that the five million dollars that he estimated this initial extension

would require would not cost New York taxpayers a single cent. He would raise the money from private investors. And, he promised that all of the work would be done underground with almost no disruption to what went on in the streets above.

Beach submitted his request with the firm belief that even with Tweed's shadow hanging over them, the legislators, so impressed by what the subway promised to do for New York, would approve an application that they knew the Boss opposed. And he was right. With unusual speed, the lawmakers approved the application and granted Beach the right to begin extending his subway.

When news of the legislature's vote reached Beach, he was ecstatic. Not only would he now have the opportunity to build the unique transit system that he was convinced would save the city, but he would be able to recoup the more than $350,000 of his own money that he had spent in building his demonstration line. But his joy was short-lived.

Both Beach and the legislature had underestimated Tweed's ability to get whatever he wanted accomplished and whatever he opposed defeated. Once it was approved by the legislature, only one thing could revoke Beach's newly acquired charter. That was a veto of the legislature's vote by the governor of New York. At the time, New York's governor was John T. Hoffman, a politician totally controlled by Tweed. Hoffman not only vetoed Beach's bill, but also signed another bill that had been proposed by none other than Tweed. Known as the Viaduct Plan, it called for the building of a number of elevated railroad lines mounted above the streets on 40-foot-high stone arches. The estimated cost of Tweed's plan was 80 million dollars. And unlike Beach's subway proposal, all of this money would be taken from the public treasury, in other words, paid for by New York's taxpayers (providing yet another way for Tweed to steal millions of dollars).

In this cartoon, Thomas Nast employed two of the symbols he often used in portraying Boss Tweed—a money bag as his head, representing his greed, and his huge diamond pin, representing the wealth he had accumulated.

Almost immediately after Hoffman's actions, the legislature went back into session in an attempt to override the governor's veto. But their effort failed, and Beach was denied the charter that he had believed was in his grasp.

In almost every way, William Marcy Tweed and Alfred Ely Beach were as different as two men could be. But there was one trait they shared in common. Both were driven by a determination that far exceeded that of ordinary people. Disappointed as he was by his reversal of fortune, Beach refused to admit defeat. He would, he decided, seek more support for his subway from the public and the press, so much support that the legislature would be given enough ammunition to take another vote that he hoped would override the governor's veto.

He began by creating a petition to the legislature calling for the extension of the subway. He then placed copies in convenient places in the subway where they could be signed by the thousands of people who continued to ride his demonstration line. Thousands signed the petition; others took copies away with them and got them signed by relatives, friends, coworkers, or anyone who shared their belief in the value of the subway to New York.

Then, through articles he wrote, Beach made a direct appeal to the press and the public in general. "It is only by an elevated or underground railway that rapid transit can be realized in New York . . . " wrote Beach. "The elevated road is inevitably an obstruction, in whatever street it is built, for it is simply an immense bridge, which no one wants before his doors. On the other hand the underground railway is entirely out of sight and disturbs no one . . . "

Along with the articles, Beach took every opportunity he could to talk to anyone he believed might be able to convince the state legislature to consider his extension application again and to vote in strong enough numbers to override Governor Hoffman's veto. But as the months wore on, even the determined Beach seemed at times to be losing confidence. Then something totally unexpected took place.

In July 1871, a disgruntled New York county bookkeeper suddenly showed up at the offices of the *New York Times* carrying a large pile of the county's official records. The records, he informed *Times* editors, provided undisputable proof of the extraordinary scale of Boss Tweed's corruption and the amount of money he had stolen at public expense. It was the first time that such concrete evidence had surfaced. And it was startling. Contained in the records was the documented proof of the millions of dollars being siphoned out of the County Courthouse project into Tweed and his cronies' pockets. Here was the evidence of the other enormous sums that Tweed had illegally received in kickbacks while serving in every one of his elected and appointed positions.

Among the millions of people who were shocked by the continuing series of articles in the *Times* was an artist who worked for *Harper's Weekly*. His name was Thomas Nast, and although he was only 24, he was the most famous cartoonist in America. Inspired by the *Times's* editorials and stories, Nast went after Tweed with a vengeance. In cartoon after cartoon, he depicted Tweed and his cronies as vulgar, money-grabbing thieves of the worst kind, and he called upon the government to bring them to justice.

From the moment that the first *New York Times* articles had appeared, "Boss Tweed" had become furious. But he was even more concerned about Nast's attacks. Confronting *Harper's Weekly's* editor, he stated angrily, "I don't care a straw for your newspaper articles, my constituents don't know how to read, but they can't help seeing them damned pictures." He meant Nast's cartoons.

By this time, the *Times's* articles and Nast's cartoons had so captured the attention of a now outraged public that local newspapers throughout New York State joined in on the attack. They were joined by some unlikely allies. Other politicians jealous of Tweed's power—or angry with him for not including them in his payoffs—now found the courage to call for him to be put into prison.

On Friday, October 27, 1871, William Marcy Tweed, the most powerful man that New York had ever known, was arrested. It would take authorities two years to prepare their complex case against him, but finally he was brought to trial and convicted

During his cartooning career, Thomas Nast created the universally accepted image of Santa Claus. He also created the image of the donkey as the symbol of the Democratic Party and the elephant as a symbol of the Republican Party.

of fraud and corruption. On November 19, 1873, he was sentenced to 12 years in jail. Tweed immediately appealed, and a higher court reduced the sentence to one year.

For Alfred Beach, the downfall of Boss Tweed was nothing short of a miracle. And his spirits were even further buoyed when, as a result of the *Times* articles, the Nast cartoons, and Tweed's imprisonment, New Yorkers in the November 1872 elections voted most of the city officials beholden to Tweed, including Governor Hoffman, out of office. Almost immediately Beach reapplied for his subway extension charter. With the fear of Tweed and his cronies removed, the legislature overwhelmingly approved his application. Shortly after the legislature's vote, New York's new governor, John Dix, a strong supporter of the subway, signed the bill into law. At long last, Beach had official permission to build a passenger subway and to begin extending it throughout New York.

In this cartoon, Thomas Nast portrayed Boss Tweed as a figure much too large to be held successfully in jail.

Beach was, of course, delighted by such support, but he knew that he still had a challenge ahead of him. He had to raise the money to build the subway. But he was confident that this final challenge would be met. The greatest battles, particularly those posed by Tweed and his henchmen, had been won. What he did not know was that he was about to lose the war.

Just weeks after the Pneumatic Bill was passed, the United States suffered the greatest economic depression it had ever faced, brought on in great measure by the financial collapse of one of the nation's biggest railroads and the banks that supported it. With alarming speed, businesses went bankrupt, other banks failed, jobs vanished, and investors lost millions of dollars in the stock market. Nowhere were the effects of the depression felt more keenly than in New York City, the nation's financial capital. Within months, 25 percent of New York's workers found themselves unemployed. The nation's most vibrant and confident city became filled with homeless and hungry people.

For Alfred Beach, what came to be known as the Panic of 1873 was the death knell of his pneumatic subway. Many of the investors whom he had already lined up for the project were among the hardest hit. In a time when most citizens were struggling for survival, the last thing on their minds was support for a subway.

The Panic of 1873 lasted for a full four years, with its effects lingering for at least ten years more. By the time the nation recovered, Beach was physically and emotionally broken. His charter was worthless, and he had no choice but to close down his subway. For a time he rented out the tunnel, first as a shooting gallery and then as a wine cellar. Finally he ordered the subway sealed and forgotten. Commenting on the final days before the subway was abandoned, the New York Transit Museum has written, "On some nights, a lone figure could be seen in the vault . . . perched on a wine crate staring into the dark. It was Beach, still dreaming of the impossible."

And what about Tweed? Did his imprisonment mean the end of his evildoing? Or would the man they called Boss be able to pick up where he left off once he had completed his year in jail? Would he once again be able to line his own pockets by dashing the dreams of honest men like Alfred Beach?

Tweed certainly thought so. But almost immediately after he was released, he was arrested on charges brought against him by a number of businesses hoping to get some of the money he had extorted from them. Once again, Boss Tweed found himself in jail.

For the man who was used to doing what he wanted to do, whenever he wanted to do it, it was too much. Resorting to the tactic that had gained him so much of his fortune, Tweed bribed several of the prison guards with huge sums

A huge crowd gathers in front of a New York City bank during the Panic of 1893, each person hoping to withdraw their savings before the money runs out.

Buried under West Broadway and Warren streets (circled on the map above), Alfred Beach's sealed tunnel was quietly and too quickly forgotten as a vast city grew up, around, and over it.

of money and was allowed to escape. Aided by other well-paid accomplices, he eventually made his way to Spain, where he planned to spend the rest of his life in luxurious hiding.

It was a daring plan—but it didn't work. Once in Spain, Tweed was spotted by a man who recognized him from Nast's cartoons. Immediately arrested, he was placed on an American naval vessel, brought back to the United States, and put back in prison. This time there would be no escape. Totally defeated and completely disheartened by the news that many of his former cronies were preparing to testify against him in return for lighter sentences, Tweed's health began to fail. On April 12, 1878, the man who had once attracted crowds wherever he went died alone in a prison cell.

NEW YORK GETS ITS SUBWAY

ALFRED BEACH DID NOT LIVE TO SEE A SUBWAY BUILT IN NEW YORK. HE DIED in 1897, a time when congestion in the city was worse than ever. Millions of immigrants from nations around the globe were pouring into New York seeking new lives and new opportunities. Tens of thousands of Americans from other parts of the nation continued to move into the city. By the late 1880s, New York was one of the most crowded places on Earth.

By this time, new types of transportation systems had been introduced. There was the elevated railway carrying passengers above the city streets on tracks supported by enormous girders. But, as Beach had predicted earlier, the railway blocked out the sun on the streets beneath it, forcing those who worked or lived under the El, as it was called, to spend their days without sunlight. Electricity had also been invented, and New York had one of the nation's largest electric trolley systems. But even though the trolley represented the best means of urban transportation yet devised, there were soon so many trolleys in New York that the streets were as clogged as when Beach had first envisioned his subway. There were many who increasingly came to believe that Beach had been right. A subway was the only answer. Ironically, it took an act of nature to get things started.

By the late 1880s, when this photograph was taken, New York's streets were more congested than ever, and there were still no plans for building a subway.

When New Yorkers awoke on the morning of March 12, 1888, they were greeted by an astonishing sight. Just two days earlier they had been basking in warm temperatures, but now their thermometers read well below zero. A raging blizzard was underway, and the city was rapidly being buried in drifts driven by hurricane-force winds.

Amazingly, tens of thousands of people still set out for work. Probably this was because they were New Yorkers, accustomed to dealing with all the challenges of life in the overcrowded, still-growing city. How could a mere blizzard keep them from carrying out their work?

They were dead wrong. By noon the city was covered with almost four feet of snow, and the storm showed no sign of letting up. The electric and horse-drawn trolleys were brought to a standstill. Scores of men and women, forced to try to fight their way home through the bitter cold and the enormous snow drifts, suffered heart attacks and died. Others were electrocuted when they stepped on fallen wires that were buried beneath the snow. Still others were killed when they were struck by tree limbs, signs, or other heavy objects propelled by the unrelenting winds.

The hordes of people who attempted to make their way home on New York's elevated railway found themselves in a particularly dangerous situation. One by one, the cars on all four of the Els were forced to a halt by the snow, stranding more than 15,000 people high above the city. Aware that the stranded passengers faced the real possibility of freezing to death, many young men risked their own lives by hoisting ladders up to the cars and carrying passengers to safety. Other young men had a different motive. They too raised ladders up to the cars, but then informed passengers that they would only bring them down if they paid the unscrupulous "rescuers" a 25-dollar fee.

In all, more than 400 people died in the blizzard. The shock that the disaster caused played a major role in forcing city officials to at last take action to build a subway system that would not only solve the congestion problem that Alfred Beach had tried to conquer, but also make it safe for New Yorkers

The Blizzard of '88 was so enormous that huge mounds of snow remained in many places in the city throughout the entire summer. Outside there were still three-foot drifts as late as mid-July.

to travel within their city no matter what nature had to offer.

Within weeks of the calamity, the mayor of New York formally proposed the building of a subway. Still, it took six more years for the opposition to the construction of such a system to be overcome, opposition based mainly on the fear that the tunneling that would have to take place under the streets of New York would weaken the foundations of the city's largest buildings. The result, some people proclaimed, would be a disaster even greater than the Blizzard of '88.

But thanks in great measure to the persistence of New York mayor Abram Hewitt, the subway at last gained final approval. Still, a major question remained. Who would finance the enormous project? The answer came in the form of

August Belmont, one of the nation's richest individuals and a man both in love with his city and a firm believer in the importance of a subway.

And there was another vital question. Who would be the chief engineer? Who had the ability and courage to take on the enormous task of designing a subway to run under the world's largest and busiest city and to oversee its construction? To August Belmont, there was only one man for the job, and that man was William Barclay Parsons.

Still only 35, about the same age that Beach had been when he began building his subway, Parsons had already been involved in engineering projects around the world, including the building of a railroad in China. He believed that engineering was the noblest of all professions and was fond of quoting Archimedes, the father of engineering, who centuries ago had stated, "Give me a lever and I'll move the world." The New York subway, Parsons felt, would not only assure the greatness of New York, but also be his crowning achievement.

Prior to becoming the man responsible for building New York's subway, William Parsons had served as chief of engineers for the U.S. Army during the Spanish-American War.

For the next six years, Parsons worked night and day determining a plan for what would be the world's largest and most advanced subway. He began by traveling to Europe, where he spent weeks studying the workings of the London subway system. Most of the London cars were still pulled by steam locomotives, but what truly fascinated Parsons was an experimental stretch of the line that was powered by the recently developed "miracle of electricity." From London he went on to Paris, where, upon encountering the design for the subway that city was planning to build, he discovered that it was to be powered totally by electricity. Before returning to America, Parsons made his first major decision. Even though it would require an electric plant far larger than any that had ever been built, the New York subway would be electrically powered.

In the following years, Parsons made other important decisions. With the help of engineers working under him, he laid out a 21-mile route under the streets of New York. He decided that the subway would have four tracks.

RAPID TRANSIT WORK AT
UNION SQUARE, June 8th 1901
Copyright By

This photograph of the subway construction at New York's busy Union Square shows how the tunnel was dug close to the surface before the tracks were laid and a tunnel roof constructed.

Cars traveling on the outer two would make local stops at 19 different stations. The two inner tracks would carry express cars making only three stops along the route.

With this settled upon, Parsons had one final major decision to make. How far under the earth should the tunnel be dug? From the beginning, he, like Beach before him, was aware that many people, while highly in favor of the subway, were frightened by the prospect of traveling deep underground. Because of this, he decided on what was called a "cut and cover" method of tunnel building. He would build his tunnel by cutting through the pavement of the streets and digging a trench fairly close to the surface. Then a steel frame for the tunnel would be erected, the tracks would be laid down, and the trench would be covered up.

It was, Parsons believed, a solid plan, but he knew that it was filled with tremendous challenges. First of all, in a time before steam shovels and bulldozers had been fully developed, most of the backbreaking work of removing thousands of tons of earth and other obstacles would have to be done by hand. The great majority of the more than 7,700 workers would be Italian and German immigrants, Irish Americans, and African Americans, almost none of whom had ever been involved in digging a tunnel. The dangerous job of dynamiting through the miles of solid rock that lay beneath the city's streets would be carried out by miners who would be hired from around the country. They were, on the whole, a hard-drinking and often unruly lot, and Parsons knew that keeping them in line would be a particular challenge.

By March 14, 1900, Parsons felt that everything was in place for the

Workmen waterproof the subway floor.

construction of the subway to begin. It did not take long for the workers and the engineers to realize that, if anything, they had underestimated the enormity of the task. The first thing they discovered was that the land that lay beneath the city presented unexpected obstacles. As the digging progressed they found that, along with the solid rock that had to be dynamited, there were underground streams and even quicksand with which they had to contend.

Building the tunnel also meant ripping out the miles of water pipes, the sewers, and the increasing number of telephone and electrical wires that lay beneath the streets in the path of the subway. Once removed, they had to be repositioned in

Directly under City Hall, this photograph shows the vaulted ceilings and decorative tilework that remain a feature of the New York City subway today.

different locations. The greatest challenge of all had to do with the fact that the route of the subway took it out of Manhattan into Brooklyn. This meant constructing that section of the tunnel under the East River. Very few tunnels had ever been built underwater, and for weeks laborers working on the section were frustrated in their efforts to effectively dig their way through the riverbed. Parsons finally solved that problem by bringing in hydraulic shields modeled after the one that Alfred Beach had invented.

The disruptions to the city during the more than four years of construction were unlike anything any metropolis had ever experienced. "The embarrassments which [New York City] landmarks have suffered during the exigencies of the subway construction," wrote *Century Magazine*, "were plain to anyone who . . . crossed Union Square where [the statue of George Washington] spent the summer pointing majestically to a tool shanty and a pile of steel columns, while the rear legs of [Washington's] horse were standing on the brink of a forty-foot chasm."

The building of the tunnel took place simultaneously all along the 21-mile route, and every section of the city was literally torn apart. There were stone crushers, tool sheds, and workers on almost every corner, blocking the streets and filling the city with relentless noise and dust. Worst of all for most citizens was the dynamiting that went on day and night. Store owners complained that their merchandise was continually being knocked off their shelves by the blasts. Homeowners railed against the fact that their windows were constantly being blown out. Many buildings, as opponents of the subway had warned, collapsed from the concussions and were destroyed.

But with it all, the construction moved relentlessly forward. And, given the magnitude of the project and the constant dangers, it was inevitable that serious accidents would take place. Before the subway was finally completed, thousands were injured and at least 45 people were killed. The most spectacular of these accidents occurred when a wooden shed in which 200 pounds of dynamite was stored caught fire and exploded. The blast, which seriously damaged the Murray Hill Hotel, shook Grand Central Station, shattered all the glass in buildings for blocks, killed five people, and injured 125 others. Reporting on the explosion, the *New York Times* called it "The most violent in point of noise, force and widespread destruction that has occurred in the United States from any cause."

"No person or beast seems safe from the prospect of disaster," reported *Century Magazine.* "Horses have fallen clear to the bottom of the subway ditch and have been hoisted out unhurt; others have not been so lucky. People have fallen in many times, and burglars have jumped in and escaped their pursuers."

Along with the hundreds of accidents, there were what could only be regarded as miracles. Marshall Mahey was working in a compressed air tunnel under the East River when it collapsed. Mahey was jettisoned out of the tunnel by the force of the compressed air but somehow survived. "I closed my eyes," he later recounted, "and managed to get my hands over my head when I realized I was in sand and was being pushed by a tremendous force. I was being squeezed tighter than any girl had ever held me and the pressure was all over me, especially on my head . . . the last thing I recalled was seeing the Brooklyn Bridge while I was whirling around in the air!"

Given all the disruptions and all the challenges that had to be overcome, the

Throughout the entire
construction of their
city's subway, New
York business owners
and residents lived in
constant fear that their
neighborhood might be
next to suffer a serious
street collapse such as the
one shown here.

87

This cutaway etching from 1911 shows the multiple levels of the subway transportation system.

greatest miracle of all, in the opinion of many, was that the building of the subway was accomplished. But it was. On October 27, 1904, the New York subway was ready to receive passengers, and the entire city conducted a celebration. Sounds of the horns from the hundreds of ships in the East River filled the air. Church bells rang from one end of Manhattan to the other. City officials in formal attire greeted the crowds who were anxious to be among the first to see for themselves if New York's horrific traffic problems had, at last, been solved. It was a mad scene, far beyond anything that William Parsons could have imagined. "Indescribable scenes of crowding and confusion," reported the *New York Times*. "Men fought, kicked, and pummeled each other in their mad desire to reach the subway ticket offices. Women were dragged out either screaming in hysterics or in a

This illustrator
appropriately titled the
drawing "Step Lively."
From the moment it
opened, the New York
subway became one of
the city's busiest places.

swooning condition." That first night, more than 100,000 people paid the five-cent fare and went underground to ride the subway. Many dressed up for the occasion and held special subway parties.

Alfred Beach had been right. From the moment it opened, the new subway transformed New York. Within the first week of its opening, ridership on the vehicles that had so clogged New York's streets dropped 75 percent. For the foreseeable future, at least, the traffic problem that had choked the nation's greatest city had been solved by the greatest subway of them all.

The subway was, in fact, such a success that within three years new construction was started on lines that would carry passengers to even more locations throughout the city. As workers dug beneath the streets for these extensions, they, like those who had dug the original lines, made fascinating discoveries. The original workmen had uncovered the bones of a prehistoric mastodon. They had also unearthed the beautifully carved hull of a Dutch ship that had sunk in 1613. But the greatest discovery of all was to come.

In 1912 workmen, digging an extension of the Broadway line, suddenly hit upon a solidly built steel and brick wall. Breaking through the wall, they found themselves inside Alfred Beach's pneumatic tunnel. What was even more amazing was the incredible condition the tunnel and Beach's elegant waiting station were still in. Beach's subway car still sat on the tracks, although most of the parts made of wood had rotted away. The magnificent waiting room fountain still stood tall. Farther down the tunnel, the workmen found the hydraulic shield with which Beach had revolutionized the art of digging tunnels.

Today, such a historic find would result in all of the objects discovered being removed and placed in a museum for future generations to study and appreciate. But in 1912 no such action was taken. The waiting station, the car, and the hydraulic shield all remain buried beneath the city. There they sit, permanently hidden from view, standing in silent testament to one man's

Alfred Beach's tunnel was uncovered, however briefly, in 1912.

Now taken for granted, this modern subway stop at 42nd Street would not have been possible if not for the imagination of Alfred Ely Beach.

dream of a subway that would transform the nation's greatest city and change the entire notion of mass urban transportation.

He was a true visionary, but, unlike many visionaries, Alfred Beach was far from simply a dreamer. He pioneered the art of tunneling. The magazine he established became one of the world's most respected and successful scientific journals. He invented the typewriter and perfected the pneumatic tube. His hydraulic shield has been used in scores of tunneling projects, including the building of New York's mammoth tunnel linking that city with New Jersey. Above all else, Beach was a man ahead of his time. And, as history has taught us, no great advancements in technology, or in most other fields for that matter, have been possible without individuals like Alfred Beach pointing out the way.

FURTHER READING

BOOKS

Ackerman, Kenneth. *Boss Tweed*. New York: Carroll and Graff, 2005.

Burns, Ric and Sanders, James. *New York: An Illustrated History*. New York: Knopf, 2003.

Burrows, Edwin and Wallace, Mike. *Gotham: A History of New York City to 1898*. New York: Oxford University Press, 1999.

Dunbar, David and Jackson, Kenneth. *Empire City: New York Through the Centuries*. New York: Columbia University Press, 2002.

Fischler, Stan. *Subways of the World*. Minneapolis: MBI, 2000.

Heller, Vivian and the New York Transit Museum. *The City Beneath Us: Building the New York City Subways*. New York: W.W. Norton, 2004.

Pflueger, Linda. *Thomas Nast, Political Cartoonist*. Berkeley Heights, New Jersey: Enslow, 2000.

Sandler, Martin. *Straphanging in the USA*. New York: Oxford University Press, 2003.

WEB SITES

http://www.pbs.org/wgbh/amex/technology/nyunderground/
http://www.klaatu.org/klaatu11.html
http://www.vw.vccs.edu/vwhansd/HIS122/Tweed.html
http://www.spartacus.schoolnet.co.uk/USAnast.htm

SOURCES

Page 7

"The streets are alive with business . . . to a post." *New York: An Illustrated History*, Burns et al, Knopf, 2003

"It is the desire of every American . . . nation" *New York: An Illustrated History*, Burns et al, Knopf, 2003

Page 8

"It is spacious and magnificent . . . or old" *The Diary of Philip Mead Howe*, Dodd, Mead, 1927

"The entrances to these hotels . . . American metropolis" *Empire City*, Jackson and Dunbar eds. Columbia University Press, 2002

Page 8/9

"I meant to make people . . . Museum." *Struggles and Triumphs or Recollections of P. T. Barnum*, Warren Jackson and Co. 1873

Page 10

"The Erie Canal well . . . of great moneyed expectations." *Advanced American History*, Century Co., 1921

Pages 11/12
"New York is essentially . . . United States." *Empire City,* Jackson and Dunbar eds, Columbia University Press, 2002

Page 12
"Who does not know . . . New World?" *New York: An Illustrated History,* Burns et al, Knopf, 2003

"The throng and rustle of traffic . . . London." *Gotham: A History of New York City to 1898,* Oxford, 1999

Page 13
"The multitudinous omnibus . . . traffic." *Empire City,* Jackson and Dunbar eds. Columbia University Press, 2002

Page 14
"You cannot ride . . . four hours and a half." *Mark Twain: A Life,* Free Press, 2005

Page 17
"Under maximum traffic conditions . . . New York." *The Epic of New York City,* Kodansha America, 1997
"Pack the traffic of . . . dead-lock." *Empire City,* Jackson and Dunbar eds. Columbia University Press, 2002

Page 21
"The saucy machine . . . gathered." *Life in America,* Marshall Davidson, Houghton Mifflin, 1951

Pages 34/35
"This immense blower . . . per minute." *Illustrated Description of the Broadway Underground Railway,* Beach, W. S. Green, 1870

Page 37
"A tube, car, a revolving fan . . . required." *The Pneumatic Dispatch,* Beach, American News Co., 1868

Page 39
"Startling novelties . . . physicians." Brennan Website (Beach Pneumatic), Chapter 2

"Swift as Areolas . . . dreams." *The Pneumatic Dispatch,* Beach, American News Co., 1868

"The most novel and attractive feature . . . traveling." *Scientific American,* June 22, 1867

"It is . . . estimated . . . five minutes." *New York Times,* September 16, 1867

Pages 41/42
"He was a natural politician . . . immigrants." *New York Times,* March 11, 2005

"A healthy boon companion . . . boys." *New York Times,* March 11, 2005

"He had an abounding vitality . . . swaggering away." *The Great Bridge,* American Experience

Pages 55/56
"In applying Mr. Dixon's . . . unsurpassed." *The Pneumatic Dispatch,* Beach, American News Co., 1868

Page 58
"Warren Street, as stated yesterday . . . them." *New York Tribune,* December 29, 1869

Page 59
"Something has been said . . . nonsense." *New York Times,* January 5, 1870

Page 61
"The oldest inhabitant . . . swarm." *New York Tribune,* December 29, 1869

Page 62
"Our original intention . . . to its merits." *New York Times* and *New York Tribune,* January 8, 1870

Page 63
"Proposed underground . . . great bore exposed." *New York Herald,* February 27, 1870

"The opening was . . . friends and supporters." *New York Times,* February 27, 1870

"The committee . . . surprise." *New York Times,* February 27, 1870

"The problem of tunneling Broadway . . . so far." *Evening Mail,* February 16, 1870

Pages 63/65
"Different [papers] will . . . enterprise." *Sunday Mercury,* February 27, 1870

Page 65
"A remarkable work . . . manner." *Frank Leslie's Illustrated Newspaper,* February 19, 1870
"Any description . . . outlay." *World,* February 27, 1870

Page 65/66

"Certainly . . . running apparatus." *New York Times*, February 27, 1870

Page 66/67

"We took our seats . . . of the day" *Illustrated Description of the Broadway Underground Railway*, Beach, W. S. Greene, 1870

Page 68

"After we had out ride . . . life out of us." *Illustrated Description of the Broadway Underground Railway*, Beach, W. S. Greene, 1870

Page 69

"So the world goes on . . . who knows?" *Youth's Companion*, cited in Frank Delaire's, *Lost Subways*, Internet

Page 73

"It is only by an elevated . . . disturbs no one." *Illustrated Description of the Broadway Underground Railway*, Beach, W.S. Greene, 1870

Page 74

"I don't care a straw . . . damned pictures." *National Archives Learning Curve*, Internet

Page 76

"On some nights . . . impossible." *The City Beneath Us*,

New York Transit Museum, 2004

Page 85

"The embarrassments . . . . forty-foot chasm." *Century Magazine*, October, 1902

Page 86

"I closed my eyes . . . in the air." *The City Beneath Us*, New York Transit Museum, 2004

Page 88

"Indescribable sciences . . . swooning condition." *New York Underground*, PBS American Experience, 2006

ILLUSTRATION CREDITS

All images from the Library of Congress unless otherwise noted.

6, 50, 60, 84, 85, 88: © New York Public Library; 17, 58: © The Granger Collection, NY; 30, 33, 38, 48, 49: The Pneumatic Dispatch, Alfred E. Beach, NY, 1868, courtesy of Martin W. Sandler; 32, 77: © Hulton Archive/Getty Images; 34: © Courtesy of the Dresser Roots Company; 62, 65, 67, 70, 90 (all): © Joseph Brennan; 81: © Bettmann/Corbis; 91: © Shutterstock.

INDEX

Boldface indicates illustrations.

A

American Institute Fair, New
    York 37–39, **38,** 55

B

Barnum, P. T. 8–10
Barnum's American Museum,
    New York, N.Y. 8–10, **9**
Beach, Alfred Ely **18**
    accomplishments 91
    and "Boss" Tweed 48–49, 71,
        72–73, 75
    concern with New York City
        traffic 19, 27, 29
    death 79
    determination 73
    elevated railroad plan 29
    inventions 26–27, 31–32,
        52, 91
    New York Sun (newspaper)
        19, 25
    Pneumatic Dispatch **32, 48**
    pneumatic mail system **48,**
        49, **49**
    Scientific American (maga
        zine) 19–20, 22–23, 55–56
    Scientific American Patent
        Agency 23–25, 26–27
    subway car design 35, **36**
    subway challenges 29–31,
        33–34, 51, 52
    subway demonstration tube
        37–39, **38**
    subway extension 69, 71–72,
        73, 75
    subway opening reception 62,
        63
    subway plans 29
    subway power source 33–35,
        34
    subway secrecy 51–52, 58–59
    subway tunnel 90, **90**
    subway tunnel digging 55,
        56–57, **58**
    subway waiting room 35, 37
Beach, Fred 56
Belmont, August 82
Blindness 27
Blizzards 80, **81**
Broadway, New York, N.Y. **50**
    depressed pavement 58–59
    traffic jams 17
    underground pneumatic tube
        charter 49
Brower, Abraham 13
Buses 13–14, **15,** 17

C

Cable cars 26–27
Clark, J. Latimer 31
Clinton, DeWitt 10
Cooper, James Fenimore 11
Crystal Palace Exhibition,
    England 31–32, 33

D

Department stores 8
Depression, economic 75–76
Devlin's Clothing Store, New
    York, N.Y. **50,** 52, **53,** 61
Dix, John 75
Dixon, John
    letter to newspapers 62–63

supervising tunnel
    construction **58,** 64
tunnel fortification
    55–56, **57**
Doctorow, E. L. 42

E

East River, New York
    tunnel 85, 86
Economics 75–76
Edison, Thomas Alva
    24–25, **25**
Elevated railroads 29, 79,
    80
Erie Canal, New York 10,
    10–11

F

Farm technology 20–21,
    21

H

Hewitt, Abram 81
Hoffman, John T. 72–73,
    75
Horsecars 14, **15,** 16, 17
Hotels 8
Howe, Elias 21
Hydraulic shield 52, 55,
    56, 85, 90

L

London, England
    subway 29–31, 82
    tunnels **28**

M

Mahey, Marshall 86
Manufacturing 10–11
Manure 14, 16
Marble Palace, New York, N.Y.
    8
Morse, Samuel F. B. 21
Munn, Oscar 19–20, 23

N

Nast, Thomas 74, **74**
    cartoons by **72, 75**
New York, N.Y.
    harbor 11, **12**
    map 77
    The New York Sun 19, 25
Noise pollution 16–17

O

Omnibuses 13–14, **15,** 17

P

Panic of 1873 76, **76**
Paris, France subway 82
Parsons, William **82,** 82–85
Patents **22,** 23–25, 26–27
Phonograph 25
Pickpockets **16**
Pneumatic tubes
    demonstrations **30–31,**
        31–32, **32, 38,** 38–39
    mail delivery 31, 38–39
    railways 31–32, **32, 33, 38,**
        38–39
Porter, Rufus 19–20

R

Railroads
    elevated 29, 79, 80
    pickpockets **16**
Rammell, Thomas
    pneumatic railway 32
    pneumatic tube **30–31,** 31

S

Scientific American (magazine)
    articles **22, 23,** 39, 55–56
    focus 22–23
    sale to Beach and Munn
        19–20
Scientific American Patent
    Agency 23–25, 26–27
Sewing machines 21, 24
Shipping 10–11
Sholes, Christopher 27
Steam-driven transportation
    21–22, 29–30
Stewart, Alexander 8
Stores 8
Subway (Beach's secret subway)
    car design 35, **36**
    challenges 29–31, 33–34, 51,
        52, 56
    detailed diagram **62**
    discovery by press 61
    extension 69, 71–72, 73, 75
    funding 71–72, 76
    opening reception 62, 63, 64
    passenger experience 66,
        68–69
    power source 33–35, **34,** 37,
        38, 63–64
    praise for 63–66
    public opening 64–65, 66,

67, 68
    secrecy 51–52, 57–59
    stations **65**
    tunnel **70,** 90, **90**
    tunnel digging 52,
        55–57, **58**
    tunnel machinery 52,
        55, 56, 85, 90
    waiting room 35, 37,
        60, 66, 90
Subway, London, England
    29–31, 82
Subway, New York, N.Y.
    construction **83,** 83–86,
        84, 89–90
    construction accidents
        86, **87**
    construction discoveries
        90
    design 82–83
    engineer 82, **82**
    extension 89–90
    funding 81–82
    levels **88**
    opening 88–89
    opposition 81
    passengers 88–89,
        88–89
    power source 82
    stations **85, 88–89, 91**
Subway, Paris, France 82

T

Tammany Hall **44,** 45, **47,**
    71
Telegraph 21
Theater 8
Traffic **9,** 12–14, **15, 78,**

79, 89
Trolleys 79, 80
Tunnels **28, 70**
    collapse 86, **87**
    construction 52, **54,** 55–57,
        58, 83–86
    construction challenges
        33, 52, 56
    dirt removal 51
    fortifications 55–56, **57**
    machinery 52, 55, 56,
        85, 90
Twain, Mark 14
Tweed, William Marcy
    "Boss" **40, 72**
    abuse of power 42, **43,**
        45–46, 47
    arrest 74–75, **75,** 76–77
    business interests
        45–46, 48–49
    death 77
    descriptions of 41–42
    elevated railroad plan 72
    political career **42,** 43,
        45–46, 47
    political influence 72, 75
    subway opposition 71,
        72
    wealth 45, 46–47
Typewriters **26–27,** 27,
    31–32

W

Western Tornado (power
    source) **34,** 34–35, 68
Whitman, Walt 11–12
Wilson, Allen 24